Praise for

"This book is an attempt to acknowledge ... . writing and propel confidence through the development of sound habits. It offers a friendly and intimate companion to the varying emotional and circumstantial challenges inherent in the writing process and provides a specific process by which to develop more competence and confidence as a writer."

—Raymond Blanton, *University of the Incarnate Word*

"If you are struggling with academic writing, you've already read the other books, and you still can't figure out how to 'fix' your problem, this book may help you understand."

—Christine Colwell, *Shenandoah University*

"I recommend this book to doctoral students and colleagues who are dedicated to writing and scholarship as an addition to their reading on the craft of writing for publication, and as an extension of their efforts to constantly enhance their research and writing productivity."

—Marilyn L. Grady, *University of Nebraska–Lincoln*

"This is a book on the academic writing process that helps to demystify that process and provides concrete strategies for dealing with the emotional side as well as the practical side of writing."

—Kevin P. Lyness, *Antioch University New England*

"This book helps the reader understand that writer's block happens to all of us and that it is not something to pathologize or internalize in a negative sense. It moves the reader to an appreciation of their vulnerabilities, but also understanding that those personality quirks can be transformed into strength when faced head on."

—Barbara L. Pazey, *University of North Texas*

"Wisdom and kindness emanate from every page of this revelatory new guidebook, where renowned academic writing coach Michelle Boyd shows us how to find our own unique approach to living the messy, rewarding process of creating scholarship. I can't recommend this book highly enough!"

—Margy Thomas, founder of *ScholarShape*

"A helpful guide to brainstorming and conquering the blank writing screen. I love the examples and the conversational writing style."

—Robert Dennis Watkins, *Idaho State University*

Becoming the
Writer You Already Are

Sara Miller McCune founded SAGE Publishing in 1965 to support the dissemination of usable knowledge and educate a global community. SAGE publishes more than 1000 journals and over 800 new books each year, spanning a wide range of subject areas. Our growing selection of library products includes archives, data, case studies and video. SAGE remains majority owned by our founder and after her lifetime will become owned by a charitable trust that secures the company's continued independence.

Los Angeles | London | New Delhi | Singapore | Washington DC | Melbourne

Becoming the Writer You Already Are

Michelle R. Boyd

InkWell Academic Writing Retreats

Los Angeles | London | New Delhi
Singapore | Washington DC | Melbourne

FOR INFORMATION:

SAGE Publications, Inc.
2455 Teller Road
Thousand Oaks, California 91320
E-mail: order@sagepub.com

SAGE Publications Ltd.
1 Oliver's Yard
55 City Road
London, EC1Y 1SP
United Kingdom

SAGE Publications India Pvt. Ltd.
B 1/I 1 Mohan Cooperative Industrial Area
Mathura Road, New Delhi 110 044
India

SAGE Publications Asia-Pacific Pte. Ltd.
18 Cross Street #10-10/11/12
China Square Central
Singapore 048423

Printed in the United States of America

Library of Congress Cataloging-in-Publication Data

Names: Boyd, Michelle R., author.

Title: Becoming the writer you already are / Michelle R. Boyd.

Description: Thousand Oaks, California : SAGE, 2023. | Includes bibliographical references and index.

Identifiers: LCCN 2022023065 | ISBN 9781483374147 (paperback) | ISBN 9781483374161 (epub) | ISBN 9781483374154 (epub) | ISBN 9781483374130 (ebook)

Subjects: LCSH: Academic writing. | Dissertations, Academic.

Classification: LCC LB2369 .B69 2023 | DDC 808.02—dc23/eng/20220707

LC record available at https://lccn.loc.gov/2022023065

This book is printed on acid-free paper.

Acquisitions Editor: Helen Salmon
Product Associate: Paloma Phelps
Production Editor: Aparajita Srivastava
Copy Editor: Integra
Typesetter: Hurix Digital
Proofreader: Dennis Webb
Cover Designer: Janet Kiesel
Marketing Manager: Victoria Velasquez

22 23 24 25 26 10 9 8 7 6 5 4 3 2 1

• Brief Table of Contents •

• Detailed Table of Contents •

• Preface •

At the time, I didn't appreciate how powerful it was—that first little sliver of doubt. How quietly it slipped into my head, that first day on Northwestern's campus, just before the start of classes. I'd gotten into several graduate programs, all of which offered me funding, and should have been feeling invincible. But as I walked beneath the canopy of trees toward the library, the only brown-skinned person around, a thought wormed its way into my head that had never before occurred to me—not once in all the time I'd been in school: What if my high school teachers were right? What if going to an HBCU hadn't prepared me? What if I wasn't good enough?

That doubt sat silently inside, biding its time. It didn't bother to announce itself—it didn't need to. Instead, it waited and grew. Every time I fumbled through a department reception, bungling an interaction with a faculty member. Every time I sat in a seminar, fumbling for something smart to say, but not understanding what everyone was talking about (and too embarrassed to ask). Every time I sat down to write a paper, struggled with what to say, and wondered why no one else in my cohort had this problem. By the time I got to prelims, the doubt had grown larger than me and converted itself from a question into an assertion. *Oh no honey*, it said, with every word I wrote. *I don't know what you were thinking. But you're definitely not good enough.*

This book is for any scholar who's ever felt that way about themselves and their writing. It's for students who began graduate school brimming with a confidence that somehow leeched out over the years. It's for faculty who are filled with dread when they think of writing—but have to hide it from both their students and their colleagues. It is especially for women of color and other marginalized scholars whose struggles with writing have prompted them to internalize the bias that others have about their ability to do exemplary research. What *Becoming* offers all of you is something I wish I'd had that first day of graduate school. It offers an explanation of why writing is so hard—for all of us. It offers an analysis of the conditions that make it harder for some than for others. And it offers a strategy for uncovering a hidden bank of knowledge you already have that can help make writing easier.

*

I wrote this book, not because there was nothing written on the topic of emotional writing blocks, but because there was quite a lot written, but very little in usable form. It was after earning tenure, exhausted from the effort, and wondering why I'd become a professor at all, that I realized this. I'd been looking at my journals from graduate school, trying to understand where things had gone awry. What caught my attention was an entry about writing. I'd been a runner-up in a writing contest, a small, insignificant one sponsored by a public radio show. And I was thrilled by it. I was thrumming with pride and delight, even though I'd won no prize and the recognition meant nothing for my life as a scholar. Reading the entry ten years later, I was shocked to realize there'd been a time in my life when I'd loved writing. And I was dismayed to realize that, in the course of achieving "success" as a scholar, I had forgotten a pleasure that had once been so essential to who I was.

In trying to understand how that could happen, I did what many of us do. I went looking for help in a book. What I found first was a vast research literature, mostly from cognitive psychologists. I eventually discovered that, as is often the case, this research confirmed what creative writers had long understood: that the frustrations with writing are not our fault but are part of a shared experience inherent to the process of writing. What I did not find was a writing guide for scholars that translated those findings into a simple summary. I did not find the stories of other scholars through which I could normalize my experience. Nor could I find an appealing, actionable strategy for facing my fears (although I found many for boosting productivity). And while I was comforted by this individual-level analysis of writing problems, it was clear that it formed only part of the picture. So I turned to academic labor studies and my training on structural inequality to better understand how writing fears are shaped by the structure and culture of the academy.

Yet it wasn't until I began my work as an academic writing coach and retreat leader that these ideas came together in the current version of the Writing Metaphor—the tool this book offers to help you understand and move through your writing challenges. Based on an assignment my writing group gave me in 2003, an article I published in 2012, and a workshop I first delivered when I founded InkWell Retreats in 2015, the Writing Metaphor can help you overcome your writing fears by helping you better understand who you are as a writer. This tool, like all of my coaching work, relies heavily on reflection; if coaching has taught me anything it's that each writer experiences the same thing differently. That is, we all struggle with the same general problems, but each of us responds to that problem in our own particular way. As a result, it's not enough for coaches and professors to offer general advice based on best practices or our personal experience—even if that experience includes publishing extensively or coaching thousands of writers. Instead, it's more useful to help scholars raise their own awareness of their writing process: to turn inward to see what's already working well for them. Therefore, *Becoming* does not provide a single model of the writing process that fits all needs; rather, it offers a single reflective tool with which you can deepen your understanding of *your* writing process. And it offers an experimental approach to trying out any new writing strategies—so you can test all writing advice (including that you find here) and begin to trust your capacity for overcoming the natural and structural challenges of writing.

*

Becoming will therefore be attractive to humanities, social science, and natural science scholars in several different scenarios. First, it will be helpful to faculty members who are teaching dissertation writing seminars. This includes advanced seminars in graduate writing, proposal writing, and dissertation preparation and completion. It also includes courses that combine methods training and writing. Second, because this book focuses on the writing process (rather than any one disciplinary genre), it is also helpful for discipline-specific courses such as "Writing for Anthropologists" or "Writing for Health Scientists." *Becoming* would also be an excellent resource for anyone advising a dissertating graduate student: It's an actionable resource, especially for those grad students not formally enrolled in dissertation writing classes but still struggling with the transition from coursework to dissertation work. Key moments when *Becoming* would help these students make progress would be after passing their prelims, while writing and defending the dissertation proposal, and while writing the dissertation. Third, this book would be especially useful for faculty members, faculty developers, and graduate students who facilitate or are members of writing support groups—especially those who are focused on helping scholars work through their emotional writing barriers. Finally, this book will be helpful for people of color, women, and any other scholar who is marked and marginalized in the academy. I wrote this book especially for you, to help you remember the writer inside you and what they're capable of. My goal was to make the book accessible, affirming, and actionable, regardless of whether it's used alone, in groups, or courses. To help with that, it includes the following features:

Narrative style: the purpose of this book is to heighten your awareness of your writing process, so you can recover and expand on solutions you already have at your fingertips. Therefore, it's written in a narrative rather than an instructional tone, to foster engagement, empathy, and reflection. Do you see yourself in the material? Can you imagine how the proposed solutions might fit your circumstances? In addition to being more fun to write, this storytelling style invites you to interrogate the material before following it.

Real scholars' stories: throughout the book, I include detailed descriptions of how scholars have experienced, struggled with, interpreted, and overcome their writing barriers. This includes published accounts, as well as conversations with private coaching clients and scholars who've attended InkWell writing retreats. I draw on these stories, not only to provide empirical and anecdotal support for the assertion that writing troubles are shared, but also because hearing others' stories is one way that we develop our own identity as writers.

Focus points: each chapter contains at least one callout box that highlights important ideas, questions, or techniques. They're offered with the recognition that you are the person who knows best how you write. And that even when you're unsure of how to move ahead, you are equipped to figure it out.

Scholars who are new to my coaching will find a problem-solving approach that combines critical intersectional analysis, interior reflection, and collective support. Scholars who have already attended InkWell workshops or retreats, especially the Unstuck workshop, will already be familiar with the Writing Metaphor. Yet you will also find a more extensive explanation of the causes of emotional writing problems, an expanded analysis of the writing process model, and a deep well of strategies you can try on your own. I hope all readers will find *Becoming* to be a comrade you can turn to, throughout your writing life. I offer it as a compass when you are starting on a new project or facing a particularly thorny phase; a friend who reminds you that you've already solved problems just like the one you're facing; and a companion who neither dismisses nor destroys your doubts, but instead walks alongside you as you remember how to face them and move forward.

• Acknowledgments •

This book was born as an assignment, given to me by my writing group nearly twenty years ago. It then blossomed into an article, which gave me my first, partial glimpse of how useful a Writing Metaphor could be for scholars struggling to write. At the encouragement of SAGE editor, Helen Salmon, it grew into a book draft. And then, it languished: from two cross-country moves in five years; from a bereavement that turned my life into before/after; from the slow, painful realization that, in going from a faculty member to a writing coach, I had inadvertently turned writing into the least pressing part of my job. But while the manuscript was flailing, the ideas themselves were growing out of control. Thanks mostly to the many scholars I worked with in workshops, retreats, and private coaching. They reminded me, over and over, that there was more to this idea than could ever be contained in a ninety-minute workshop. In short, they told me that there was a book waiting to be written *if only someone would get off their butt and write it.*

Having received the message that so many scholars believed in what *Becoming* had to say, I then relied on many, many people to finish it. That includes Heather Radke, who never let me forget that no matter my day job, I am a writer. It also includes members of my original writing group turned supper club: after I left Chicago, Badia Ahad, Lorena Garcia, and Helen Jun held my spot open for almost five years, till I had the good sense to return to them and take up my place at the dinner table. In the intervening years, I relied on the Women of Color Writing Group in Portland, Oregon: Ayako Takamori, Kim Cameron Dominguez, Maude Hines, Nadxieli Toledo Bustamante, Shirley Jackson, and Marie Lo wove a magical web of support that didn't just help me prioritize writing; it helped me navigate the delights and frustrations of being black in Portland. Nick Montgomery gave me funny, surgically precise feedback on late-stage drafts. And Erica Meiners did what she always does: helped me untie an intellectual knot, acknowledge its political implications, and find the courage to speak those implications aloud. Through it all, Margy Thomas's friendship, generosity, and sparkling insight sharpened my thinking and eased the isolation of solopreneur life. And along with my Business Buddies Adeline Koh and Helen Sword she assured, encouraged, and modeled for me that it's possible to write a book and run a business at the same time—and be proud of both.

Neither the business nor the book would have happened without the amazing women of Team InkWell—Sonya Williams, Aushlie Coles, Alex Fry, and Nuala Conneely—who kept everything running smoothly, so I could steal time to write. When I needed a break from coaching or writing, I had long, winding, revelatory conversations with Aimee Wooda to keep me laughing and grounded and hopeful about the world. Then I crossed into the /after, and Deborah Paredez saw me and my writing through in a thousand ways, including inviting me to Study Hall with Liz Emens and Georgia Lee. Every week, these three women create a container that has room for every side of me. And they feed me poetry that winds its way into my writing and my life.

I can't thank my family enough: everything I've ever done is because of what they've done for me. My mom and dad read my books! David Stevens tolerates my mood swings while I write them. And my brother Marc made sure I didn't give up on them when the writing got hard. I wish he were here to see this one.

I'm indebted to everyone at SAGE who made this process as smooth and seamless as possible and to the Metcalf Internship Program at the University of Chicago which made it possible for me to work with research assistant Bella Constantino. I am especially grateful to the reviewers who saw what this book was trying to do, far more clearly than I did. Their feedback—intimidating in number but incisive in substance—pushed me to pull out what is unique and useful about this book and carry that thread throughout the text. In doing so, they helped turn *Becoming* from an awkward teen into a young manuscript comfy in its skin. My thanks go to:

Tamara Bertrand, *Florida State University*

Raymond Blanton, *University of the Incarnate Word*

Carroll Bronson, *Cardinal Stritch University*

Sarah Croco, *University of Maryland, College Park*

Christopher Gerben, *Stanford University*

Marilyn L. Grady, *University of Nebraska–Lincoln*

Jamie Lester, *George Mason University*

Kevin P. Lyness, *Antioch University New England*

Joyce Pittman, *Drexel University*

Robert Dennis Watkins, *Idaho State University*

Andrew Zitcer, *Drexel University*

Nothing in this book would be half as useful were it not for the hundreds of scholars who have participated in InkWell's retreats and workshops. In sharing their Writing Metaphors with me, they shared, not lifeless mental constructions, but frailties, secrets, and hidden strengths. Raphaëlle Rabanes was especially generous in this respect, and this book is better because of them. They are among the many scholars, almost all women, and mostly women of color, who've shown me what it means to face your writing fears. I'm a better coach and writer because of you, and you have my unending thanks.

• About the Author •

Michelle Boyd, PhD, is the founder of InkWell Academic Writing Retreats, a transformative, retreat-based coaching company that teaches scholars to overcome their writing fears. She is also a self-described "struggling writer" whose success as an award-winning, former tenured faculty member belied the challenges she faced throughout her career as an academic. Scholars who work with Michelle call her coaching "magical," but it's not magic—it's science. Her coaching programs are rooted in research showing that each scholar has their own natural writing process and that many of their struggles come from external barriers that prevent them from recognizing, accessing, or trusting that process when they need it. Michelle has been leading retreats since 2012 when she co-founded and coached her first retreat as a faculty member. The only thing she loves more than writing is helping scholars who dread writing develop a calm, confident, sustainable writing practice.

Down but Not Out

What It Means to Be Stuck

"Be a lamp unto yourself."

–The Buddha

Commitment isn't Ana's problem. A runner and an early riser, she's carved out plenty of time in the early morning to get her writing done. It's true, she's not really alert at that hour, so she usually doesn't produce her best writing. In fact, her brain doesn't seem to get clicking until sometime after 3:00 p.m., at which point she usually has to rework whatever she did in the morning. This is especially true if she's stayed up late the night before, which she does a few times a week—often an idea hits her late at night and she scrambles to write everything down before it floats away. She knows the morning's not her best time, "but look at what the best writers do, Michelle," she says, "Kant, Hemingway, Nabokov—they all got up early." So, she does too.[1]

For her part, Pria *loves* the morning, and she's got a nice little routine to get herself going. She used to just fritter away her first hour of writing going through email or neatening up the sunroom where she works. But now she has a cup of tea, listens to three Gregory Porter songs, and plops right down in her seat. She pulls up what she worked on the day before, reviews it, and cleans it up a little before moving on. But often, an hour and a half later, Pria's writing time is up, and she finds herself feeling tired and bewildered. She's polished that last paragraph to a deep and glowing shine and reading it would make your heart sing. But she does that at every writing session, so she never creates more than a few new sentences for the following paragraph. It doesn't help that Pria's advisor is waiting for a chapter from her and has been for weeks. She can't stand the idea of disappointing him, so she keeps writing. But *she can't stand the idea of disappointing him.* So, she never writes more than that one, perfect paragraph.

Darnell, on the other hand, will do anything he can to avoid sitting down to write. He has a beautifully organized office in the basement of his house—cozy and warm; it gives him just the right amount of solitude without making him feel isolated. He turns the computer on, it's true. But he has a wide and infinitely expandable array of "set-up" activities that he likes to do before getting started. In addition to checking his email and running a few loads of laundry, he also likes to read a blog or two about writing, "just to get my juices flowing," he says. His advisor is pretty hands off "so there's no pressure there," he tells me, and then he pauses: "But sometimes it feels like I'm just out there on my own." By the time Darnell does finally settle down to write, he usually only has about twenty minutes before he has to go upstairs and help get the kids ready for school. At that point, he pours out words in a panicked rush and has no idea what to do with the material. It literally pains him to look at the confused mess of words he's produced, so he usually decides it's all trash, crumples it up, and throws it away in disgust. The next day he comes back, opens his email, and does the same thing all over again.

Ana, Pria, and Darnell are all facing the same simple, scary situation: several times a week they sit down to write, but each time they do . . . they get stuck. Some of them do exactly what the research says they should to increase their productivity: they schedule and protect their writing time; they write regularly throughout the week, and they work in a dedicated writing space. Nevertheless, each of them follows a set of steps that leaves them ultimately unproductive: Ana "writes twice," constantly redoing her work later in the afternoon. Pria begins every day by reviewing her previous work, which distracts and snares her rather than prompts her to move on to new ideas. And Darnell, after dithering away most of his writing time, creates huge amounts of material but is at a loss as to how he should process it. In each instance, they find that, despite their best efforts, they've made little progress on their work, and in some instances, find themselves behind where they were before they started. And each of them says the same thing: that it's hard to tell what's worse—how slowly they seem to make progress or how badly they feel about themselves as a result.

Some version of this scenario—where you show up, struggle to write, and seemingly have little to show for it—is familiar to many academic writers, although the form it takes is particular to each one of us. Perhaps you finish manuscripts but tend to hold on to them, revising and tweaking, missing important deadlines in your search for perfection. Maybe you are delighted by your research and overwhelmed with ideas, but unable, when you write them down, to make sense and order of what's on the page. You might be someone who delays writing until the last possible minute, then forces yourself through marathon writing sessions that leave you depleted, unsatisfied with the work, and terrified to share it. For my own part, I have little trouble getting started, but find that self-doubt worms its way into my thoughts. So I'm sometimes unable to move past the first few minutes of writing. Regardless of the specifics, the result for writers who get stuck is frustration, disappointment, and delay.

There is no way to eliminate the considerable work that academic writing requires. The nature of writing and the professional context in which academic writing takes place, means that any scholar trying to produce a manuscript is facing a lengthy and arduous process. But what makes writing even more difficult and terrifying—for these three and many academics—is that they have not thought explicitly and systematically about their writing process and how it's affected by that context. Ana, for example, has chosen the wrong time of day to do her work, in deference to a "rule" about when people should write. As a result, she works inefficiently, often repeating her writing sessions later in the day when she's feeling more generative. Pria, on the other hand, becomes especially anxious about writing when she knows that her advisor is going to see the end product and so repeats the same work over and over. And Darnell becomes immobilized when his ideas don't come out pristine and polished. In each case, the cause of their problems lies not merely in the thinking work required, but in the expectations they're responding to, their use of a process that doesn't work for them, and the fear and overwhelm they feel as a result.

This book is designed to help you uncover your *own* writing process—so you can more easily manage your writing barriers and get more satisfaction and pleasure from your writing. Writing process is nothing more than the steps you take to move from ideas in your head to words on a page. And clarity about how you do that will help you better understand how you get stuck and how to get *un*stuck and make progress on your manuscripts. This may seem unlikely because our writing process involves a bunch of decisions that seem trivial at first glance. What could it matter whether you write the first draft by hand or on the keyboard? Tackle your reader's reports alone in your office or with the buzz of quiet conversation in a café? Read yesterday's writing first or dive right into writing a new section? Choices like these can seem so insignificant, mechanical even, and you may be only dimly aware that they are choices at all. Yet small though they may seem, these steps form the building blocks of our writing process and have a significant impact on our experience of writing: they shape the challenges we face while engaged in it and influence how quickly we're able to overcome those challenges.

When trying to develop our writing process, our impulse is often to look to others for guidance. We wouldn't be scholars after all if we didn't appreciate how many of the world's problems can be solved by a good book. Yet when we turn to outside sources for help with the writing process, we're often disappointed. Universities provide minimal training in how to develop and implement a writing process. Advice from colleagues and advisors, although well-meaning, may not fit our circumstances or our method of working. And while writing guidebooks can be useful, they can also trap us in unhelpful patterns (like Pria's early morning writing) because the research says it's the "best practice." Most importantly, turning first to outside authorities to better understand our writing process robs us of the opportunity to develop our sense of professional authority—our confidence in ourselves, our mastery of our subject, and our understanding of our process. That sense of authority is a crucial but underappreciated element of our professional success and satisfaction.

Becoming suggests taking the opposite approach. That where writing is concerned, you act as a lamp unto yourself: before seeking outside guidance on what your writing process should look like, you instead begin with an inward look—to uncover the writing process you already have. There's already a writer inside of you. They are not perfect. They might not even enjoy writing all that much. And they likely don't know everything there is to know about it. But if ten years of coaching academics has taught me anything, it's that you know more than you think. That's because you already have a writing process that feels easier and more natural to you. But for reasons we'll discuss in the next chapter, that process can get buried under a mountain of anxiety, uncertainty, and overwhelm. This book offers one way to dig yourself out from under that mountain and walk toward the writer you already are. Let's get started by taking a look at what's getting in the way.

What It Means to Be Stuck

The relentless blinking of the cursor on white space; the manuscript that stays the same for weeks; the frustrated writer draped across her desk in misery; these are the images (and perhaps the memories) that tend to pop up in our heads when we think about the problems that writers face. These vivid scenes are how we often visualize writer's block—as a wretched, pitiable, and perhaps all too familiar state in which, no matter how hard you try, the words do not come. The fundamental idea behind this popular vision of writer's block is that we are at a loss for words. That we lack inspiration, or just don't know what to say. While there are certainly times when this is the challenge we're facing, this common notion of "block" is too narrow to capture the variety of difficulties we face as writers. More useful is the concept of being stuck: that is, deliberately or unintentionally doing things that keep us from moving our project forward.[2] In other words, stuck doesn't include those times when we can't quite figure out what to do: when we're having trouble organizing our thoughts or can't find the theoretical framework that makes the most sense. Those are instances when we're stumped—puzzled, and perhaps moving more slowly than we'd like—but still working at it and moving forward. Stuck, on the other hand, is when the things we're doing are preventing us from making progress.

During my time as a writing coach, I've observed at least four forms of being stuck. The first is simply **Not Writing**.[3] This differs from the traditional notion of Writer's Block, where we try to write and are unable to do so, while Not Writers do not even sit down at the desk. One of the reasons most cited by academics for Not Writing is a lack of time (Boice & Jones, 1984), and it is no wonder. Between caretaking responsibilities, course prep, classroom teaching, office hours, committee meetings, advising, and manuscript reviews, it can feel impossible to find time to write. Recent reports suggest that it's not unusual for academics to work a sixty-hour week (Morgan, 2012; Diers-Lawson, 2013; Flaherty, 2014; Roney, 2017; McKenna, 2018; Seamons, 2019). Given these circumstances, it's no surprise that many of us begin the day with the best intentions for our writing, then look up a few minutes later to see that the day is over, and we never even opened our document.

Not Writing can also afflict scholars who have plenty of time and know it. These are perhaps the most tormented Not Writers because they are often too embarrassed or ashamed to ask for help. Busy Not Writers have the "excuse" of having no time in their schedule to protect their egos. But procrastinating Not Writers—those whose homes are clean, whose closets are organized and filled, like mine is, with blankets they crocheted while avoiding their writing—those Not Writers are often grappling with a level of self-doubt and shame that can be debilitating. And the line between Not Writers who have plenty of time available and those who have none can be a very thin one indeed.

Not Writing can even afflict scholars who have a firmly established writing habit. One of the triggers of this kind of Not Writing I tend to see is when something happens that shatters a scholar's confidence so that they can't get back to writing. And given that academics write in a context of constant potential criticism, it's not unusual for this to happen. The disruptor might be a particularly harsh comment from an advisor. It might be experiencing (or even witnessing) public humiliation while giving a presentation. Damning reviews are also a common source of writing stuckness. One scholar who worked with Robert Boice explained that

> my writing was moving along nicely until the rejection of my book manuscript came. I had put my whole soul into that thing. . . . Angst is the result. I don't have the will to get back to writing, so I'm getting further and further behind where I should be. My general state of apprehension is growing day by day; once I get back to writing, the pace will have to be explosive. Still, I'm not sure, given what the reviewers said, that I can write anything outstanding. (Boice, 1994, p. 2)

The fear of rejection and disapproval is also one of the motivators behind **Side Writing**, a second way we can get stuck. Side Writing can be especially disruptive for those who are just establishing a writing habit and have been told (by people such as myself) that "anything that moves your work forward is writing." It's true that thinking, reading, analysis, note-taking, outlining, free-writing—these and other tasks that scholars routinely dismiss as "not real" writing are core, foundational writing acts. Without them, the composition of prose cannot take place. The distinction between Side Writing and moving your work forward is that Side Writing is what we do when we are *technically* writing but doing so to avoid the more challenging work required to advance the development of our ideas. In other words, Side Writing is writing in disguise—a writing-specific version of "workcrastination."

One of the clearest indications that you may be in Side Writing is that you find yourself performing the same activity over and over again. One of its most seductive forms is repeated data analysis—what scholar is not compelled by the need to rerun equations (with perhaps another variable), to double-check interpretations, to review primary sources just *one last time*? Because these acts form the basis for the ideas we're developing through our writing, scholars often perform them over and over: not necessarily to enhance their understanding of the phenomenon in question, but to calm their fears about having "missed" something. At other times Side Writing shows up as repeat revision, as with Pria who can't stop making the perfect paragraph. Unlike Not Writers or Binge Writers, who experience quite acutely the negative consequences of being stuck, Side Writers may not be aware that there's a problem until they have been writing for a fairly long time. When they do realize it, they may be confused and angry (with themselves) for the delay, even though they find it difficult to stop.

If we Don't Write or Side Write for too long, we can find ourselves in the unhappy position of **Binge Writing**, a third form of being stuck. This is the pattern of not writing for long periods, and then writing in painfully long chunks (Kellogg, 1986). It's the thirty-page seminar paper written in the twenty-four hours before it's due; it's the slowly moving download bar and the quickly ticking clock as you and everyone else researching your topic submit an online federal grant application three minutes before the deadline. The next time you board a flight to a conference, see if you can spot Binge Writing in the seats around you: it's the laptop that's snatched from the backpack, whipped open before the tray tables are down, and kept on for the duration of the flight in a tense race to finish the paper before the panel starts. Perhaps you wouldn't need to look up from your seat on the plane to spot the Binge Writer. If so, that's because you're in good company.

As Boice points out, Binge Writing is extremely unpleasant—not just because it requires long periods of work, but also because it requires "forcing," that is, compelling ourselves to write long past the point when we want to or are producing anything of much worth. This is a key difference between Binge Writing and falling into Flow. Both can be marked by hyperfocus, a sense that we are totally "in" the writing. But while Flow feels effortless and energized, binging—especially when we do it to meet a deadline—is a grueling, white-knuckle experience. Both forcing and binging, Boice tells us, are damaging strategies, which take much more than they give. His research shows that both "decrease the likelihood of writing again the next day or next week. Both, in the long run, lead to less output and less satisfaction in writing, less quality and originality in the product, and fewer successes with editors than do more temperate, regular schedules of writing" (Boice, 1994, p. 4).

It makes sense that Binge Writing diminishes the quality of our writing. Whatever your natural rhythm, pace, and process for clarifying your ideas, Binge Writing makes that intolerable. Because it is frequently motivated by our need to meet a deadline, Binge Writing necessarily elevates quantity over quality, production over content. It steals away the time we need to think through ideas, pore over implications or contemplate the fit of a single word.[4] In the face of an impending deadline, such considerations become secondary to just getting out something that is less humiliating than the thing you wrote just a few hours before. As I will illustrate in Chapter 5, this no-nonsense, outcome-oriented mode of thinking is actually useful when refining an essentially finished work. But if we are not yet at that stage of a project, then rushed, forced writing can damage our manuscript.

In short, the problem with getting stuck isn't just (or even, primarily) that it impacts our writing productivity. The more serious problem with getting stuck is it affects the *quality* of our work and our work experience. When we're stuck in Not, Side, and Binge Writing, we're unable to do what's necessary to fully develop our thinking. Messiness and confusion are a natural part of writing. And it's not unusual to find ourselves with plenty of ideas that we're unable to assemble in a way that makes sense. Bolton and Rowland refer to this as "writing chaos" and point out that

> all writing, particularly academic, has times when it seems a complete muddle with no possible order, ever. There is so much wildly disparate and dislocated stuff, and yet it all has to have a proper place in the publication. (2014, p. 58)

If we're stuck, we don't have room for the natural, inescapable moments when we do not understand our thoughts and must labor through the process of becoming clear to ourselves.

In addition, these forms of being stuck diminish our capacity for producing elegant prose. Since we are not, as scholars, known for our graceful and readable style, we might not initially be concerned about that. Yet, as Stephen Pyne points out, style is not "merely decorative or ornamental, any more than are feathers on a bird. Style performs work. Whatever its loveliness or ostentation, it is what allows the creature to fly, to attract mates, to hide from predators, to be what it is" (Pyne, 2009, p. 10). In other words, style directly influences the clarity and impact of our arguments (Pyne, 2009; Narayan, 2012; Sword, 2012). When writing is rushed, there is no time to consider this seemingly less important element of writing, much less to use it to strengthen our arguments. What gets lost, as a result, is the specificity of our terms, the precision of our arguments, and the clarity and significance of our conclusions.

The last form of stuck that I'll mention is **Endless Writing**. Kissing cousin to Side Writing, Endless Writing is what happens when scholars just can't let our work go. It's what we do when the thought of other people seeing our work is so abhorrent that we cannot bring ourselves to initiate the most important stage of the writing process—the moment when we share our ideas with others.

It does not pay to rank the evil wrought by these forms of being stuck. Whichever one you are experiencing at the moment is likely to feel like the worst one, and may the heavens help you if you're experiencing more than one at a time. Together they can seem like the Four Horsemen of the Academic Apocalypse, a thundering quartet of ruination, each one delivering its own exquisite form of suffering. *Not Writing* ultimately does the most straightforward damage for scholars whose promotion and tenure depend on publication.

Without writing, none of the material, psychological, and reputational rewards of traditional institutions are available to those scholars. *Endless Writing*, though, is the most tragic. Those who suffer from it often have everything you'd want in a piece of scholarship: deeply researched, complex, beautifully rendered ideas that, while imperfect, would nevertheless make a rich contribution if only they were released into the world. *Side Writing* is the heartbreaker, a charming, sugar-tongued liar who allows you to fool yourself until it's too late.

But of all the forms of being stuck, *Binge Writing* is the most pernicious. Like *Side Writing*, its disadvantages are hidden until long after they've begun to make their mark. Binge Writing is a habit that can be maintained over many years and is even appreciated as a sign of true professional commitment and intellectual grit. But the truth is, its slow, sly deterioration of our natural approach to writing can eventually makes us hate the whole process and sap our passion for the thing we once loved.

Flow and Forward Writing

Biblical harbingers of Conquest, War, Famine, and Death might seem a bit histrionic to those who have never been stuck in their writing. More troubling is the fact that some of you may be reading these words and thinking to yourself that I have not described being stuck but have merely described writing itself. "If not for the writer's Four Horsemen," you might be asking, "Then what?"

There are two alternatives that writers can aim for. The first is what psychologist Mihaly Csikszentmihalyi calls **Flow**. Flow is that magical moment when everything works. When the words come easily and ideas slip together, seemingly of their own accord. It's those times when the entire frame of an argument becomes magically, radically clear to us. So we steal a few minutes just to get it all down—then look up and find an hour has passed. Csikszentmihalyi explains that Flow is

> what the sailor holding a tight course feels when the wind whips through her hair, when the boat lunges through the waves like a colt—sails, hull, wind, and sea humming a harmony that vibrates in the sailor's veins. (1990, p. 3)

In other words, Flow is that strange combination of tightly focused attention and completely open awareness that makes us feel, not just connected to, but totally in tune with the writing. In moments like these, our ideas fall so neatly into place, we can almost hear them clicking together as we write. Flow doesn't happen every time we write—but we can learn certain strategies that prime us for falling into Flow and increase the ease with which we're able to do so (Perry, 1999). Yet even the most skillful, prolific writers do not experience this all the time. And if we imagine Flow to be the only acceptable alternative to Stuck, we will be disappointed.

Another kind of writing we can shoot for is **Forward Writing**. Forward Writing is the regular, steady, and (usually) incremental development of your project, through the articulation, elaboration, clarification, or support of your ideas. Forward Writing pushes you past where you were when you sat down to work, but it does not look the same each time it happens. It might involve writing a certain number of words or pages per day, but often it does not. At the beginning of a project, Forward Writing might take five minutes and involve sketching a mind map on a napkin, with cryptic notes that only you can understand. It can happen serendipitously and, in a flash, while you're sitting on the floor of the library, reading a book you happened upon while drifting down the stack to see if any nearby titles look useful. Forward Writing might be that one sentence, crafted with a delicacy and precision you've been aiming at for years, that begins "In this book, I argue that..." Forward Writing might also be the seventeen hours it takes you to reread your entire dissertation, with that one sentence argument by your side on an index card, checking to make sure that each paragraph, each section, and each chapter is working to support that argument.

Sometimes, Forward Writing is the painful, paradoxical realization that everything you have been writing has gone utterly off course, and you must now cut the bulk of your argument. This writing has become a pet of yours, despite its irrelevance and the damage it does to your argument. But as poet and essayist Annie Dillard (1989) rightly insists,

> This writing weakens the work. You must demolish the work and start over. You can save some of the sentences, like bricks. It will be a miracle if you can save some of the paragraphs, no matter how excellent in themselves or hard-won. You can waste a year worrying about it, or you can get it over with now. (Are you a woman, or a mouse?) (1989, p. 4)

Forward Writing, then, is not magic, although when we're lucky, it can feel, like Csikszentmihalyi's flow, quite magical. Often, however, writing is mundane. Perhaps tedious. Sometimes painful. And very often, Forward Writing is mysterious. "When you write," Dillard suggests that

> you lay out a line of words. The line of words is a miner's pick, a woodcarver's gouge, a surgeon's probe. You wield it, and it digs a path you follow. Soon you have found yourself in deep new territory. Is it a dead end, or have you located the real subject? You will know tomorrow, or this time next year. (Dillard, 1989, p. 3)

Dillard elegantly asserts a fundamental truth: that even Forward Writing is difficult. That it is a creative process, one over which we have only partial control.

Scholars do not, as a profession, tend to spend much time on the idea that the work we're engaged in does not bend to our will alone. Instead, we tend to maintain a false division between scholarship and so-called creative writing, between intellect and imagination. Yet we experience the incoherence and unwieldiness of the creative process each time we sit and write, whether the words flow like butter, or refuse to come at all. In the face of this mystery, then, amid a process that can only be coaxed and never fully controlled, how do we keep from getting stuck? How do we find our way to Forwarding Writing?

The Promise of Writing Process

Many academic writing guidebooks point out that our writing problems come from our failure to write regularly—a problem that can be solved by productivity and time management protocols. Thanks to this work, we know that scheduling shorter, more frequent writing sessions, telling someone what we plan to accomplish, and then telling them what happened all make it more likely that we'll establish and stick to a regular writing schedule. These works have helped countless scholars plan their writing projects (Zerubavel, 1999; Rockquemore & Laszloffy, 2008), write regularly (Boice, 1990; Gray, 2005; Silvia, 2007; Jensen, 2017; Sword, 2017), learn the conventions of academic writing (Belcher, 2009; Goodson, 2013; Hayot, 2014), and develop accountability measures to support them through the creation of the manuscript (Silvia, 2007). This literature has given us a much clearer idea of the strategies that are most likely to help us show up for writing and have developed crucial insights into a profession that has all but ignored the topic for years. What this literature is less clear on is what to do once we've shown up for our writing.

Becoming picks up where that work left off. Drawing on the research on writing barriers, as well as my work coaching and leading writing retreats for academics, this book examines why writing feels so scary and immobilizing. And it explores how we can increase the chances that we will dive into writing—even when doing so feels terrifying. It suggests that one reason academic writing is so challenging is that the conditions under which scholars work encourage us to forgo, rather than follow our natural writing process. So one way we can move from fearful to Forward Writing is to uncover our process and learn to trust it. To help with that work, I offer a single reflective tool—the Writing Metaphor—that you can use to explore and elaborate your particular writing process and determine which strategies will fit how you work.

Understanding our writing process can't eliminate all the challenges we face. Some are inherent to our writing experience, while others are ingrained in academic culture and social hierarchy. So, we can expect these challenges to remain with us regardless of age, experience, or seniority. But knowing one's process can help change our relationship with those challenges: the way we *think* about them; the way we *feel* about them; and the way we *behave* when they pop up. Once we understand and, more importantly, trust our process, we have a greater chance of facing and moving past those challenges, instead of running away from them. We might still feel uncomfortable when those challenges arise. But we'll be less likely to be derailed by them when they do.

Becoming is not the first work to consider the emotional and psychological barriers of academic writing—in fact, it gratefully draws on those books to offer the analysis I give here.[5] Yet it differs from those books in three key ways. First, its ultimate purpose is not to boost your productivity. It's possible that what you read here *will* help you publish more quickly. But if it does so, that will be a secondary effect. The true aim of this book is to expand your sense of ownership of the writing process: to cultivate the awareness that your writing belongs to you. And to strengthen your sense that you have the right and the capacity to make good decisions about the process you use and the ideas you communicate. The stronger your sense that your writing belongs to you, the more writing becomes your route to professional security: to greater pleasure. To deeper excitement about your research. To the simple comfort that comes from not panicking every time you sit down to write.

The second way *Becoming* differs from other work is that it sees following one's process as an act of power. In an environment where writing is the gateway to most of the symbolic and material rewards of our profession, the work that once excited us—thinking and talking about ideas and how they can change us and the world—can easily devolve into a competition for approval. Writing can get reduced to something we "have to do to get tenure." And the joys of intellectual play—making mistakes, exploring dead ends, and pursuing outrageous claims—become too risky to engage in because they threaten our professional reputation and progress. Yet despite these circumstances, *Becoming* suggests that it's possible to reclaim your writing as a practice of freedom. That each time we honor our writing process, we refuse the conditions and logic that make writing so terrifying. And that, paradoxically, doing so will make scholars more, not less likely to meet institutional demands for writing productivity.

Finally, *Becoming* differs from other writing guides in that it does not recommend any particular "best practice." Instead, it offers a reflective tool to help you better understand yourself as a writer—so that you can then better understand which "best practice" is best for you. In taking this approach, I am strongly influenced by the work of scholars such as Kamler and Thomson who suggest that the true solution to helping scholars successfully navigate the hurdles of writing is to "[move] beyond a focus on tools and techniques to the discursive practices of becoming a scholar" (2008, p. 507). *Becoming* tries to do so by demonstrating that, no matter where you are in your scholarly life, it is useful to first turn inward to discern what you need to enjoy and complete your work.

My hope is that *Becoming* will serve, not as a writing guide, but as a writer's companion. That it will accompany you as you come to understand who you are as a writer and a scholar. I have tried to create, as well as I can in book form, the sense of warm, supportive companionship I always see among scholars when I lead a writing retreat—a feeling that depends in part on scholars' willingness to share their stories with one another. Therefore, you will find stories and insights from a wide range of scholars—some from published accounts and some from scholars I've coached—all describing the emotional and psychological blocks that get in their way, as well as the writing process they use to move past them.[6] I rely on these generously shared stories, not just to illustrate writing challenges and solutions. But more importantly, to remind you that you are not alone: that we are all struggling through this Herculean task alongside one another. And that whatever your burden or worry about writing, it is shared by someone else. I encourage you to share these stories—and your own—with others. And return to them, for comfort and courage, throughout your writing life.

Chapter Overview: From Problem to Puzzle

While going through this book, I invite you to think of writing as a puzzle rather than a problem: a thorny, maddening one at times—no doubt. But also, one whose solution generates an unbeatable feeling of beauty, pleasure, and satisfaction. To help you do so, Chapter 2 begins by asking not "What's wrong?" but "What's happening?" It shows that writing isn't just a matter of simply transcribing our cleanly worked-out thoughts. Rather, it's a complex, unwieldy process that is more difficult to master than we initially think. And as much as we might dislike it, stumbling is a natural part of that process. "So what?" you might wonder. "Who cares what's happening when I write?" My experience coaching academics suggests that knowing why writing is difficult provides us with the intellectual armor—that is, the conceptual language and framework—for analyzing rather than pathologizing our writing struggles. Once we understand the nature of the challenge we are facing, it is much easier to address.

Having provided some clarity (or confirmation) of what's happening when we write, Chapter 3 asks "What could happen instead?" It answers that question by elaborating on the concept of writing process. In describing its stages I include examples from a wide range of scholars to show how unique the writing process is to each person, as well as how following your process helps you get past the emotional, technical, and strategic challenges described in the previous chapter. I hope that you'll finish this chapter with a clearer sense of the "big picture" of any writing project and the ability to identify where *you* are in your projects at any given time.

Chapter 4 is where we dive into the work of uncovering your particular writing process. It's here that I describe the tool of the Writing Metaphor and walk you through the steps of developing your own. Doing so is like taking the bare sketch of yourself outlined in Chapter 3 and filling it in with detail, shade, and color. The Writing Metaphor takes the generalized model of the writing process and makes it your own, by revealing what you're already doing as a writer that feels natural and helps you move past challenges. Be prepared: The Writing Metaphor will also reveal what's *not* working for you and often give you insight into why. At this point, it will be tempting to judge, criticize, and ask yourself "How do I fix this?"

I encourage you to maintain your sense of writing as a puzzle, not a problem, and ask yourself instead, "How might I handle this?" That's the question we tackle in Chapter 5, which describes a method for experimenting with different strategies to see which ones fit and enhance the way you work. It also provides several strategies with which you can experiment. After reading this chapter, you'll have a method for incorporating new elements into your writing process while staying grounded in the core approach that forms who you are as a writer. You'll also have a treasure trove of strategies you can return to and experiment with, whenever you find yourself stuck in the future.

The work this book asks of you isn't easy. It requires time, space, and quiet—exactly the conditions academic institutions make difficult to find. So Chapter 6 concludes by describing how to develop an oppositional writer's consciousness and use it to create relationships that make it easier to brave the risks of writing.

Solving the Writing Puzzle: How to Use This Book

Solving the puzzles that your writing presents will be much easier if you endeavor to adopt three habits of mind while reading this book: the first is a *spirit of experimentation*. I can promise you that some of these exercises when you first read them and consider them abstractly will seem silly and perhaps even painful. I can also promise you that if you only *think* about them (and how silly they are) they are not likely to help you at all. In describing how professionals make successful changes in their careers, Herminia Ibarra argues that "we learn who we are—in practice, not in theory—by testing reality...We discover the true possibilities by doing" (Ibarra, 2004, p. xii). Similarly, I suggest that the best way to learn who you are as a writer is to actively and fully engage in the exercises.

The second habit of mind that will come in handy while reading this book is *kindness*. If your response to that last sentence is to wince inwardly, I promise you, you are not alone in your discomfort. One trait I have observed in virtually every writer I have worked with is an unrelenting tendency to judge and punish themselves before they understand. This sharp impatience is not surprising, given that academia valorizes criticism and conflict as the best routes toward knowledge production. However, in this instance, such an approach merely gets in the way. It is, in fact, a weakness, because it prevents true discernment—the ability to see what is happening and imagine alternative possibilities. Working with your Writing Metaphor will affirm what's working for you and will also point out what's *not* working. So it can tempt you toward self-judgment. It's essential therefore that you treat yourself the way you treat your students: with the kind expectation that, of course, you don't already know everything there is to know. If this approach seems ridiculous, useless, or just plain pathetic, my suggestion is to be kind to yourself secretly and temporarily, while reading this book—no one will be the wiser.

The final habit of mind that will support you while you read *Becoming* is one that I hope you will grow over time, as you experiment with the ideas in this book. That skill is **trust**. I have yet to work with a writer who did not have some intuitive sense of what worked for them and what did not. It's typically when they ignore that intuition, and instead, try to adhere to external expectations unrelated to their process that they run into the most difficulty. This book asks you to pay attention to what you are telling yourself. It asks you to respect the intuition that is so central to knowledge discovery—and your success as a scholar—and apply it to your writing life.

Focus Point

1. Many writing challenges are the result of looking to others for writing guidance instead of following our writing process.

2. We're stuck in our writing when we inadvertently or knowingly do things that prevent us from making progress.

3. Being stuck looks different for different scholars at different times.

4. Writing progress isn't always an unimpeded forward movement. Instead, it can also be slow, multidirectional, and uncertain.

Notes

1. See Popova, M. (2015, October 5). *Famous writers' sleep habits vs. literary productivity, visualized*. The Margina. Last Retrieved April 4, 2022, from https://www.themarginalian.org/2013/12/16/writers-wakeup-times-literary-productivity-visualization/

2. In general scholars agree that writer's block involves "the inability to begin or continue writing" (Rose, 1984, 3). But there is still some debate about what writer's block looks like—that is, whether certain behaviors (e.g., procrastination) are an instance of blocking or its cause (see Ahmed, 2019). There is also the occasional assertion that writer's block isn't a real problem, at least not for academics (Silvia, 2007, 45–47). I use the term "stuck"—the one I hear most often from my coaching clients—to describe the wide range of conditions that keep them from writing and cause them to seek out support.

3. Not Writing, as I describe it here, is different from Murray's NotWriting (Hjortshoj, 35–38 referencing Murray), which Murray describes as an essential period of waiting before one begins writing. See Murray, D. M. (1992). *Read to Write: A Writing Process Reader.* Holt, Rinehart, and Winston.

4. While I describe this condition as deadline driven, upon rereading, it strikes me that this is what it feels like to try to meet publication requirements in general.

5. Recent work by Sword (2017) and Zumbrunn (2021) are among the most helpful of these and forthcoming work by Sword (2023) promises to add to the bounty.

6. These descriptions and stories are taken from my writing retreats, writing workshops, and private coaching clients. Except when indicated, I have changed minor details, names, and identifying information in order to protect their confidentiality.

More Than You Think

How Head, Hand, and Heart Make Writing So Hard

"The struggle is inner: Chicano, *indio*, American Indian, *mojado*, *mexicano*, immigrant Latino, Anglo in power, working class Anglo, Black, Asian . . . The struggle has always been inner, and is played out in outer terrains. Awareness of our situation must come before inner changes, which in turn come before changes in society. Nothing happens in the 'real' world unless it first happens in the images in our heads."

–Gloria Anzaldúa

When I ask Pria what bothers her the most about getting stuck, she doesn't mention her slow progress. What bothers her most is that this behavior—this incessant revising of the same perfect paragraph—seems so unlike her. She's highly organized and usually manages challenges with hard work and persistence. So she's confused and frustrated by her inability to overcome this problem. "It just doesn't make sense," she says. "That's not the writer I usually am."

Pria is like many of my coaching clients—people who have long seen themselves (and been seen by others) as "a good writer," but are now finding themselves stuck in a way they can't understand. Perhaps they sailed through undergraduate coursework with a string of all-nighters. Or, they have a long history of banging out well-received conference papers just hours before they are due. They may have even had a rock-solid record of steady, incremental progress—but now they can barely bring themselves to look in their office, much less sit down and open up the manuscript. They get that writing is challenging. What they don't understand is how "challenging" has turned into "impossible."

The truth is, though, that having trouble with writing actually makes complete sense. Even for a full professor with decades of experience and an eighty-page CV, scholarly writing is an incredibly demanding task, one whose cognitive, technical, and emotional demands most scholars have never been taught to recognize, much less manage. Even scholars who study writing are challenged by it: "Writing never came easily," says education professor Mike Sharples. "I still wrestle with words as if they were opponents that must be strangled into submission" (1999, p. xi). In making this admission, Sharples names himself as one of a large group of top scholars who find writing to be arduous (Anzaldúa, 2003; Forester, 1984). Happily, he is also one of a large group of top scholars who have spent their time explaining to us how we get stuck. And what they tell us is that writing isn't just hard—it's filled with difficulty and delay.

It's helpful to think of writing challenges as taking three separate forms—they are Inherent, Institutional, and Interpretive. Inherent difficulties are just part of the writing process. They come with the territory if you want to write. Institutional challenges are those produced or exacerbated by the structure and culture of the academy. They might *seem* natural, or at least inescapable. But they are the result of choices, pressures, and patterns that are communicated and reinforced by the organizations in which many scholars work. Finally, Interpretive challenges are those that arise from how we understand and explain our experience of writing to ourselves. The pattern I've long observed as a coach is supported by anecdotal and empirical evidence: We get stuck in our writing when we misinterpret Inherent and Institutional writing challenges as, not just our fault, but fundamentally indicative of our incapacity as individuals. Interpretive challenges require the inner work of which Anzaldúa speaks in the opening epigraph. If we want to get unstuck, it helps to understand, not just the writing; not just the context in which we do the writing; but also how we interpret both. The way in which we reinterpret *ourselves* in the context of both.

If you're feeling particularly desperate about the state of your writing, you might be tempted to skip a chapter on why we get stuck and move to the ones that are more focused on what to do about it. But our misreading of what's happening when we write is one of the key factors keeping us from being able to successfully negotiate its difficulties. It's precisely our failure to accurately recognize, name, and analyze writing challenges that keeps us from developing effective responses—ones that are suited to our particular circumstances, approaches, and capacity. Gaining this understanding does not magically eliminate the difficulties of writing. Yet the struggle becomes more manageable when we correctly diagnose its sources.

To do so, we'll begin by examining the inherent challenges of writing. Then we'll look at how the structure of academic institutions transforms writing from merely difficult to risky, generating anxiety as well as self-doubt. Next, I'll describe how we respond to that risk by interpreting it in personal instead of in contextual terms. Finally, I conclude by previewing how learning to trust our process can help us get unstuck.

Actually . . . It *Is* Hard: The Inherent Challenge of Writing

"Writing is hard for every last one of us" says writer Cheryl Strayed. "Coal mining is harder. Do you think miners stand around all day talking about how hard it is to mine for coal? They do not. They simply dig" (Strayed, 2012, p. 60). With characteristic hard-nosed empathy, Strayed conveys the silent assumption of many academics: writing may be difficult, but it's not hard enough to complain about. And it's certainly not hard enough to justify getting stuck (Black et al. from Antoniou and Moriarty, 2008, p. 208; Silvia, 2007; Barreca, 2011).

True enough: Writing—especially the writing done by scholars—is not dirty, dangerous, poorly paid manual labor foisted on people with few alternatives.[1] It is nevertheless an incredibly demanding task, one whose many dimensions we often cannot see. To better understand what's happening when we can't write, it helps to understand that writing is *inherently* challenging. That is, regardless of how you generally feel about writing, or how well any individual writing session may go, setbacks and uncertainty are part of the writing experience. Most importantly, those challenges aren't just intellectual. To get a fuller picture of how we get stuck, it's helpful to recognize that Inherent writing challenges involve the Head, the Hand, and the Heart.

The first set of writing challenges resides in the Head because writing is a cognitive task that is far more demanding than most of us realize. Of course, as scholars, we understand that thinking is hard work. But we don't always appreciate all the mental processing involved—or give ourselves credit for how tiring that work can be. The second set of writing challenges resides in the Hand: in other words, writing "like an academic" is a technical skill, and like any other, it requires constant learning and refinement as we go through our careers.[2] The third set of challenges resides in the Heart: That's because the work of navigating the first two dimensions of writing is emotionally taxing. Trying to express our ideas in the format and voice required by our disciplines can raise our fears, threaten our professional identity, and make us doubt our self-worth. And very few graduate training or mentoring programs explicitly or systematically prepare scholars for the emotional aspect of writing. This way of thinking about writing highlights the fact that writing—and its challenges—are something we experience as a whole human being. So if we want to move past those challenges, we have to see and care for the whole human being as well.

Watch Your Head: The Cognitive Demands of Writing

To get a clear sense of how cognitively demanding writing is, it's helpful to remember the research of psychologists Torrance and Galbraith. They remind us that to accomplish even the simplest of writing exercises, your brain must complete and switch between a dizzying array of complex tasks, including:

> monitoring the thematic coherence of the text; searching for and retrieving relevant content; identifying lexical terms associated with this content; formulating syntactic structure; inflecting words to give them the necessary morphology; monitoring for the appropriate register; ensuring that intended new text is tied into the immediately preceding text in a way that maintains cohesion; formulating and executing motor plans for the keystrokes that will form the text on the screen; establishing the extent to which the just generated clause or sentence moves the text as a whole nearer to the intended goal, and revising goals in the light of new ideas cued by the just performed text. (2008, p. 67)

Put more plainly, even when we have a fairly clear idea of where we are going with our argument, the act of "figuring it out" involves (to name a few things) remembering and hunting for the idea itself, either in our memory or in some recorded document, selecting the words required to express that idea, and placing those words in an order that makes sense internally, as well as in relation to the words that come before and after them. Our brain must also direct our fingers, hands, and arms to move in whatever way will make letters appear on our screens and pages. And of course, we have to make sure the idea fits with the overall message of the work and change it if it doesn't. In other words, the task we think of as simply "figuring out what we want to say" is anything but simple.

To make matters even more complex, figuring out *what* we want to say is just one of two major cognitive tasks we are engaged in while writing. A second major task is figuring out *how* we want to say it—that is, how the point we are making should be organized so that our audience will accept, understand, and be convinced by it (Hyland, 2008). I say more about this in the next section, but for now, it's important to note that, because of this cognitive task, we're constantly moving back and forth between those two considerations (what to say and how to say it) to make sure we're on the right track. Sharples refers to this back and forth activity as a "cycle of engagement and reflection" (Sharples, 1999, p. 7). When we're absorbed in our writing, Sharples explains, we are

> [d]evoting full mental resources to transforming a chain of associated ideas into written text. At some point, the writer will stop and bring the current state of the task into conscious attention, as a mental representation to be explored and transformed. Often this transition comes about because of a breakdown in the flow of ideas into words. It might be due

to some outside interruption, a noise, or reaching the end of a sheet of paper, or it might be because the mental process falters: the ideas fail to materialise or the words stop in mid-sentence. The result is a period of reflection. (Sharples, 1999, pp. 7–8)

The Cycle of Engagement and Reflection neatly captures the fact that we do not plow relentlessly ahead when writing, a torrent of words cascading from mind to fingers to page in a steady flow. Instead, we turn on the faucet and then turn it off to see what lies in our sink. Nothing. So we swish around the contents. We decide we need more warm water, then turn the corresponding spigot. We do this over and over, whether we're writing an email to a colleague or crafting the discussion section of an article. In other words, stopping and starting, writing and checking, confidence, then questioning—these disruptions are all a natural part of the process.[3]

What this means is that writing is not merely challenging. Rather, writing, by its very nature, involves breakdown, detour, delay, and failure. When we question whether we've clearly expressed ourselves; when we return to what we've written to ensure we said what we meant to; when we agonize over our failure to neatly capture and convey the essence of a finding or interpretation; when we get off track, cannot remember our point, or find that we have landed in a place that is neither what we actually think nor the logical extension of the beginning of our argument—all these twists and turns are in fact *what writing* is. This process of trying, questioning, hesitating, rejecting, and starting over—none of it reflects our inadequacy as writers. Rather, going through these moments is an indication that we're doing exactly the right thing. The stops and sputters are inherent to the act of writing itself.

Take Me by the Hand: The Mastery That Never Comes

In addition to being cognitively demanding, writing is also a technically challenging task, one that puts us repeatedly in the role of a novice writer, even as we move forward in our careers. The term "novice writer" isn't my euphemism for a graduate student. Rather, I use the term to describe anyone who is actively learning the conventions of whatever writing genre they are attempting at the moment, regardless of their rank or experience.

As a profession, we have a strange relationship with the notion of academic writing genres. On the one hand, we implicitly acknowledge their existence, since we understand that the structure of scholarly writing differs from that of other forms of writing. On the other hand, we rarely use the word genre when discussing our work. Worse still, we are not always given explicit training in the genre we are expected to master. Instead, graduate students often feel that professors assume their understanding of their field's genre conventions (Ciampa & Wolfe, 2019). They characterize the process of writing a dissertation as "an independent adventure" and describe having to read other dissertations, "to gain a deeper and greater perspective of what this chapter is supposed to look and sound like in the end" (Ciampa & Wolfe, 2019, p. 93). As one scholar put it, it feels as though "you're supposed to know all about it, you're supposed to achieve a standard that's not discussed but expected" (Fergie et al., 2011).

Mastering academic genres involves learning at least two things. The first is what the relevant structure is; the second is how to use that structure so well that we can achieve the required logical or analytical task. A novelist who writes about a young mother's suicide, for example, might need to master the conventional story structure of exposition, rising action, climax, falling action, and denouement. But they must also write in a way that draws the reader in emotionally and convinces them to suspend disbelief.

Likewise, a sociology student writing a dissertation proposal to examine the causes of suicide among young mothers will need to write an introduction, literature review, methods, findings, and discussion section. But they must do so in a way that convinces their committee that the study adds something to the vast storehouse of knowledge that already exists on the question at hand. This is why the skillful use of genre is important: our correct use of genre improves our ability to convince our reader of our argument. How? Hyland asserts that in correctly using genre, we are sending an unspoken message that we understand and are adept at the techniques that other scholars find compelling. In other words, the heart of academic persuasion is

> writers' attempts to anticipate possible negative reactions to their claims. To do this they must display familiarity with the persuasive practices of their disciplines, encoding ideas, employing warrants, and framing arguments in ways that their potential audience will find most convincing. (2008, pp. 3–4)

Such familiarity does not happen overnight. Instead, like a sophisticated research method or a deft hand at teaching, writing "is a craft, a skill that needs to be learned. There is nothing innate about writing, there is no gift and so it has to be worked at" (Carnell et al., 2008, p. 12).

Although I have dwelled here on the example of graduate students, they are not alone in facing this problem: the same process of slow mastery of new writing forms exists throughout a scholar's career and is part of the process of professional growth. As Carnell et al. (2008) learn from their interviews of scholarly writers, the developmental process "is continual. Although they have 'arrived' as successful published authors, the writers describe a lasting state of thinking about writing and learning about writing" (2008, p. 14).

Consider, for example, that after you have finally had a proposal accepted by your committee, you may then be required to write a dissertation, which, depending on your discipline, may be the first draft of a book of several hundred pages, with a strong, well-supported argument that is carried through each chapter, something entirely different from the seminar and conference papers you have written up to this point.[4] If you are lucky, someone will expect, at some point, that you convert that dissertation into a job talk, and then into either a series of articles or a book. Once you have figured out what is supposed to go in the book proposal (and how to modify that template proposal to fit the sometimes widely varying requirements of each press), you revise the dissertation and publish a book. From there, you will need to write a "book talk," which is similar to, but distinct from a dissertation-based job talk. The kind of writing that can follow these key genres varies by discipline and rank but may include work as widely varying as meta-reviews, keynote addresses, roundtables, TED talks, and media appearances. And if you are a practitioner or activist, you may also want to learn how to better visualize your data and convert your findings into formats that are accessible to those not mired in the jargon of academia. So that, throughout your career as an academic, you can expect to *continually* encounter, misunderstand, screw up, fumble through, and then—very slowly—understand and master new writing genres.

We can also expect this learning process to be bumpy each time we go through it. That is, once we have mastered one writing genre, we cannot expect to swiftly and easily become experts in another. I, for example, have a half-written article of which I am quite fond that has never been published because as a junior faculty member, I did not understand how to fit it into the template of academic writing. As a result, I abandoned it, assuming that my idea was not fleshed out enough, or significant enough (read, not good enough) to be worth writing. It was only several years later, after the analysis was no longer relevant, that I realized that the problem was not the material, but my own inability to figure out a genre and venue more appropriate to it.

Most importantly, this article abandonment took place after I had experienced several apparent successes in my career. By the time the idea for the piece came to me, I looked on paper like an expert, someone who had "mastered" her genres. And in person, I tried mightily to live up to that impression. Yet the fact is, I was still very much a novice writer, both of conventional academic writing, and certainly of any form of writing that took an alternative format. But because I misunderstood the problem as one of quality as opposed to fit, I lost out on the opportunity to publish a novel piece on a topic I was excited about. My point is that, no matter who we are or what our relationship to the academy, it is natural that in our attempt to master new forms of writing, we will run into trouble.

Be Still My Heart: The Emotional Toll of Writing

The cognitive and technical dimensions of writing each illustrate the third challenge inherent to writing—it often generates strong emotions that are unpleasant and uncomfortable. When I ask scholars, at the beginning of a retreat, to name the part of writing they love the most, there's often a bit of shuffling. Then an awkward silence. Then one of them admits (to a chorus of murmured agreement) that they're having trouble thinking of anything they like about writing at all. When they do come up with something, one of the answers I hear most often is that their favorite part of writing is . . . finishing. Not necessarily because doing so fills them with a great sense of pride—but because the act of getting a manuscript off their plate and "into the pipeline" gives them temporary relief from the strain they felt while scrambling to get it out.

Fear that we will never finish. Shame when we reach a breaking point. Rage when someone plagiarizes our work. Guilt when we take an hour or a day off. Desperation when we realize we can't meet the deadline. Loneliness as we try to muscle through. All of these and more are what I hear scholars dealing with when writing.[5] Publicly, we tend to talk about these feelings as "writing anxiety"—a sense of impending dread when we think about having to write.[6] Sometimes these uncomfortable feelings are what keep us from writing, as we see from museum studies scholar Pam Meecham:

> I was so concerned about the process and so in awe of writers and writing that I was afraid to read my own writing. Many of the things that I wrote were not edited well enough because I didn't want to be confronted with my own work. (Carnell et al., 2008, p. 12)

Even when these feelings don't prevent us from writing, we still have to contend with them while trying to get the writing done. This is the case even for well-established professors who themselves study writing anxiety. For example, writing scholar, Mike Rose says:

> I wish I could tell you that writing is pure pleasure, that I sit down at the desk at 8 in the morning, and the next thing I know it's 5 in the evening and I've had this blissful day lost in thought. But no, it's not at all like that. If somebody had a little camera on me, and they traced out the patterns of my writing day, there would be dozens upon dozens of times when I'm getting up from the chair and going to the refrigerator, and getting up from the chair and going up for a walk, and getting up from the chair and trying desperately to think of anybody I can call. (Mike Rose from Arora, 2010)

Rose's self-deprecating description of his physical agitation is more than a lighthearted rendering of his writing troubles. It's also an apt illustration of one of the most important facts about our feelings—they are a physical phenomenon. Although we may name them in our minds and express them with our tongues, our emotions are felt in the body.

Perhaps you've sometimes felt like music education scholar, Lucy Green does when sitting down to write:

> I go to my desk in the morning and I actually feel nervous, as if I was going to go on stage and sing a song or play the piano or give a lecture. I think, "So ridiculous, Lucy, I mean nobody's going to read what you

write in this room today." . . . And yet I actually feel dry in the mouth, my heart's beating a little bit fast. It's crazy and I don't understand it. (Carnell et al., 2008, p. 37)

What Lucy describes are the classic symptoms of stress. When we encounter a threat, our bodies go through a set of neurological and physiological shifts designed to help us manage the threats. Her pounding heart and dry mouth are a response to all the chemicals being released into her system (Bane, 2012; Nagoski & Nagoski, 2020). What makes this emotional response so significant for writing isn't just that it's unpleasant. But that it can actually make it difficult to think. As sophisticated as it is, our brain doesn't distinguish well between physical threats (say, a car careening toward you as you cross the street) and social threats (the worry about "looking stupid" when you have to give a talk based on this argument you can't figure out). So when we feel fear about writing, our body goes through the same response it would if we were staring at a snarling dog: The part of the brain that takes care of writing (the cortex) sits down and the part that manages threat (the limbic system) stands up and takes charge. And "with the limbic system driving the bus . . . we are not capable of innovative, nuanced thinking. . . . None of the higher thinking functions—the frontal cortex's 'executive functions'—are available" (Bane, 2012, p. 21). In other words, just at the moment we most desperately need our brain to get us out of a jamb, the feelings we're having about the jamb itself make it difficult for our brain to perform.

I'm not suggesting that all the feelings we have about writing are negative. There is much pleasure to be found in writing and thinking—we know this, or we would never have become academics in the first place (Hitz, 2020; Sword, 2017, 2023). What I am saying is that uncomfortable, unpleasant feelings are an unavoidable part of being a writer. And you are mistaken if you believe that the writing struggles you face are proof that you are "just not cut out" for this work. Instead, quite the opposite is true. The research tells us that, when you have those feelings, "you are not being weak-willed, thin-skinned, oversensitive, underdisciplined, or lazy. You are reacting to a subconscious awareness of a potential threat" (Bane, 2012, p. 27).

Therefore, our work as writers is not to hide our fears, nor to eliminate them. Instead, our work is to accept the fact that

> writing brings with it a whole herd of psychological obstacles—rather like a woolly mass of obdurate sheep settled on the road blocking your car. For you to move forward, these creatures must be outwitted, dispersed, befriended, or herded, their impending genius somehow overcome or co-opted. (Malamud Smith, 2012, p. 5)

So far, we have thought about the three challenges of Head, Hand, and Heart separately. But, of course, what's difficult about writing is how they interact with one another, in ways that diminish our confidence.

The Whole You: Head, Hand, and Heart in Writing

We can clearly see how the three dimensions of writing interact when graduate students embark upon one of the great hurdles of graduate training: writing their dissertation literature review. As with any writing task, this one is seated in the Head, requiring the brain to search for, remember, monitor, and organize content as well as to manipulate the physical body in order to produce it. The work of the Head is complicated by the challenges of the Hand: that is, the literature review requires students to illustrate, not just subject matter expertise but mastery of the literature review genre as well.

Mastering this genre is particularly difficult, given that graduate coursework often does not clearly explain what a literature review is, or provide systematic training in how to write a strong one. In fact, it tends to do the opposite: assign seminar papers that require completely different skills than those needed to complete a lit review (Hayot, 2014, pp. 7–16). It's not surprising then, when students are understandably bamboozled into thinking that the purpose of the literature review is—as the name suggests—to survey the studies that have been done and describe their conclusions. However, a literature review isn't just a survey. It's a synthesis. One in which "diverse and sometimes conflicting ideas and findings in the literature need to be evaluated and combined to create a new, original work that provides an organized overview of the state of knowledge on a topic" (Pang, 2016, p. 1). A review that fails to do so, while it may be well organized and exhaustive, would be heavily criticized by a dissertation committee since it typically does little more than recount the studies in excruciating and inconclusive detail.

Not only do students often receive little training in how to create a literature review, but as a faculty member, I often observed in myself and my colleagues a distressing inability to clearly convey exactly what the problem was with the review before us.[7] Therefore, having long ago gleaned, mastered, and naturalized the skill of writing literature reviews, professors may inadvertently use vague language to explain what the problem is. I can remember times when, as a dissertation committee member, I worried (never aloud, but often in my head) that the student's literature review indicated that they "didn't get it," or "couldn't grasp" the nature of the intellectual enterprise. Notice how this language suggests the fault lies with the student's ability rather than their place in the learning process, or—heaven forbid—my failure as an instructor or advisor.

Once a student receives this feedback, their next draft may successfully identify the main themes in the research, as well as the stances that various groups of researchers take relative to those themes. In this instance, we inarticulate committee members may admit that the graduate student is showing a capacity to "do something with" the extant literature, as we like to say, with a vague wave of the hand. Yet even at this point, the student will be told that their review fails to make an argument about what is missing from the literature and what contribution their proposed research will make to that body of work.

It's easy to imagine what is happening with the Heart at this point, as students navigate the difficulties of the Head and the Hand. Easy to imagine how, even in the best of circumstances, they might feel frustrated, discouraged, or apprehensive. What's less easy to see is Kamler and Thomson's point that the limitations we notice in a graduate student's work often reflect, not the quality of their thinking, but their reasonably undeveloped sense of authority. Specifically, a graduate student's initial attempts at the literature review are

> frequently misunderstood as *poor writing* when what is at stake is the difficulty of writing as an authority when one does not feel authoritative. So, for example, when students write the literature review, they may describe, rather than evaluate, the work of expert scholars; they mask their own opinions and arguments with layers of *who said what about what and with what effects*, because they lack confidence and are afraid of taking a stand. (2014, p. 508)

In other words, successfully managing the cognitive, technical, and emotional challenges of the lit review depends on a graduate student feeling confident enough, not just to synthesize existing arguments or develop arguments of their own. Navigating those challenges also requires them to take up the role of expert; to judge the strength of senior scholars' research and assess the state of the field as though they have the knowledge and right to do so. As David Bartholomae points out, "all writers, in order to write, must imagine for themselves the privilege of being 'insiders'—that is, the privilege both of being inside an established and powerful discourse and of being granted a special right to speak" (Bartholomae, 1985, p. 143).[8] Yet, because junior scholars are still in the learning phase, they lack the expertise and confidence of their advisors and other more senior scholars and are therefore unable to insert that authority into their writing.

For a graduate student, performing a subject authority and community membership they neither feel nor have is difficult, even under the best of circumstances. For marginalized graduate students, it's even harder, since they are likely to have their authority stripped of them regularly. If you, like me, have had someone walk into your campus office while you're seated at your desk, stop short and say, "Oh! Do you know where Professor Boyd is?" then you understand in a visceral way what an avalanche of research has confirmed: that the authority and belonging of immigrants, women, people of color, working class, differently abled, and gender-nonconforming scholars are constantly challenged in the university. That their authority is denied in classrooms, where students assume that scholars of color are sharing their opinions rather than research findings. It is denied in evaluations where "factors including an instructor's gender, race, ethnicity, accent, sexual orientation or disability status negatively impact student ratings" (Flaherty, 2021). That authority is denied during office hours, when students demand friendship behavior from women professors, then lash out when their requests are rejected (El-Alayli et al., 2018). That authority is denied in the hiring process, which defines scholarship on marginalized bodies as irrelevant to the main concerns of the discipline. In other words, the authority that's a requirement for the successful execution of the *technical* aspects of writing is not a given. It's a privilege that is unevenly granted.

My point here is not that we should forgo multiple rounds of review or pull back on honest, constructive feedback to graduate students. My point is that we mistakenly regard writing as a relatively straightforward and doable task—as the mere transfer of our thoughts to the page. When in fact, writing is a cognitively, technically, and emotionally harrowing feat, one that requires a strong sense of professional authority and belonging that's often still under development and, for some, under attack. So if you've ever felt embarrassed for being tired after a writing session; if you've ever struggled to figure out what your editor or advisor wants your manuscript to "do" differently; if you've ever felt too timid to face another day wrangling with your manuscript, it wasn't because you were doing anything wrong. It's because you were writing. And what Cheryl Strayed said is true—writing isn't coal mining. But it *is* its own, wearying process of hacking away in the dark and cold. Of hitting dead ends and doubling back and tunneling toward an uncertain prize.

Focus Point

How does this depiction of writing problems line up with your experience? Of the three inherent challenges of writing, which has been more troubling for you: Head, Hand, or Heart?

Institutional Challenges: Running the Risk of Writing

If the inherent difficulties of writing were the only things that got in our way, we'd almost be in luck. Unfortunately, the inherent challenges of writing are exacerbated by the conditions in which scholarly work takes place. These conditions transform writing into a risky performance and test of one's worth as a scholar. Whether we write. How much we write. Whether people perceive us to be writing. And what we say when we do write. All of these influence our material welfare, our standing among our peers, and our personal well-being. We feel these risks in the classroom, at job talks, during receptions—and we feel them when we write. Therefore, it can seem like every time we sit down to write, we are risking the loss of that standing and its attendant damage to our well-being.

The concept of Writing-as-Risk is brilliantly explained by sociologist Pamela Richards in Howard Becker's classic book, *Writing for Social Scientists*. While the chapter takes the form of an informal letter from Richards to Becker, it nevertheless lays out a basic theory of risk in academic writing. Richards explains that writing is risky for scholars because it requires us to expose ourselves to scrutiny in three key ways. First, we're exposing the quality of our *writing*—that is, how well we have mastered the academic writing genres. Second, we're exposing the quality of our *ideas*: not the format in which we write, but the content of what we say. Third and most importantly, we're exposing *our identity as academics*. "If you give someone a working draft to read," Richards asserts, "what you're asking them to do is pass judgment on your ability to think sociologically. You're asking them to decide whether you are smart or not and whether or not you are a real sociologist" (Becker, 1986, p. 114).

In making this point, Richards echoes a strand of writing scholarship that asserts that writing is even more than the cognitive, technical, and emotional experience I describe in the previous sections. Rather, writing is a social practice. It is an act we engage in as part of a community and in order to gain rights to that community. Therefore, writing is risky because each time we develop an idea, make an assertion, support it with evidence, draw conclusions, and suggest implications, we are not just constructing an argument: we are asserting our "right" to enter the community of scholars, and are therefore faced with the possibility that someone might deny our entrance.

Other scholars have discussed how academia's environment of risk impacts the writer's voice (Thesen & Cooper, 2014) as well as writing productivity and practice (Hjortshoj, 2001; Berg & Seeber, 2016; Sword, 2017). It's also the case that these risky conditions impact the *process* of writing—that is, what scholars do in the moment of our writing session to get our ideas out on the page. That happens because these risks are not merely something we experience during presentation or publication. Instead, we experience the risk in the act of writing itself. As one scholar puts it,

> Ultimately you know that you're writing for something for publication. Therefore people are going to read it and you don't know who they are or where they'll be and what they'll say about it or what they'll think about it and so you are exposing yourself. Even though you're sitting in your room, now you're deferring the public appearance which will be only, not your face, but a black-and-white version of you. So I suppose that's what makes you nervous. (Carnell et al., 2008, p. 12)

In other words, worries about what our colleagues will think don't arise only when we're presenting, or even submitting our work. These worries also arise when we're deciding which word to use, what article to cite, how to frame a problem, and even what problem to consider. The "black-and-white version of you" is a specter that can haunt even the most senior scholars.

Sources of Risk

There are three key features of scholars' professional context that can make writing feel particularly risky. The first is a hypercompetitive job market, which, as Richards explains, positions graduate students and colleagues as competitors during and after the job search process. Specifically, "the discipline is organized in a way that undermines . . . trust at every turn. Your peers are competing with you psychologically . . . and structurally. Tenure, grants, goodies are becoming more and more part of a zero-sum game, as the academic world feels the current academic crunch" (Becker, 1986, p. 115). While Richards is speaking specifically about the field of sociology more than thirty years ago, her words ring true for academia as a whole, and the trends she notes have become even more exacerbated since she first wrote these words.

The clearest example of this hypercompetition is the severe gap between the number of PhDs and the number of tenure-track jobs available. In 2018, only 27 percent of faculty positions were tenure track (AAUP, 2018). This means that 73 percent of the faculty jobs held by PhDs were adjunct positions without adequate pay, security, benefits, protections, and long-term prospects (American Federation of Teachers, 2020). Given the limited number of secure positions available, it's not surprising then, that the National Science Foundation's Biennial survey showed that from 1997 to 2017, the percentage of PhDs holding a tenured or tenure-track position decreased in the engineering, math, computer, health, physical, earth, and life sciences, as well as in psychology and the social sciences (Langin, 2019). And in a 2014 analysis, Larson et al. estimated that of the few tenure-track positions available in the United States, only 12.8 percent of PhD graduates could expect to earn one (Larson, Ghaffarzadegan, & Xue, 2013).

Not only are you competing for fewer positions, but once you do earn one, you'll likely be expected to publish both earlier in your career and at higher rates than scholars who came before you. Universities have doubled down on a business model that measures productivity almost exclusively in terms of the number of manuscripts a scholar publishes[9] (Mountz et al., 2015; Berg & Seeber, 2016). As a result, you are likely experiencing what is essentially a work speed up—a demand that you produce more, sometimes without increased pay. In 2019 for example, sociologist John Robert Warren examined the top programs in his field and found that new assistant professors today have published twice as much as their counterparts did twenty years ago. His study also showed that associate professors who focused on articles "published almost twice as many articles as their counterparts in the 1990s." Even scholars who focused on books increased their article output—publishing as many articles now as article-focused scholars produced in the 1990s (Warren, 2019, p. 182). Similar findings have been reported in other disciplines (Pennycook & Thompson, 2018). And there's some evidence that the demand for increased publication has also increased at liberal arts colleges (Reinero, 2019). This situation—where jobs are few and uncertain and the work required is enormous—is often seen as new and a function of the recent corporatization of academia. Yet as Nzinga and others point out, scholars whose work challenges the traditional notion of the canon have long labored under a subtler form of job scarcity—because they do not fit racialized and gendered notions of "real" scholarship (Nzinga, 2020, p. 57).

These conditions make writing especially risky because they change the stakes of writing. Job scarcity means that writing isn't just the way we express complicated ideas to ourselves and others. Job scarcity means that writing is *also* the activity we engage in to establish and defend our financial stability in a profession that has secure jobs for fewer than 30 percent of those who are trained for them. Few scholars I work with talk about loose labor markets or work intensification. Instead, they say "If I don't finish this book I'm not going to get tenure." They say "What if I missed something and somebody notices during the job talk?" In other words, they name the concrete moment during the job acquisition and tenure process when the quality of their writing will weaken or destroy their job prospects.

These conditions are worrying enough for scholars working from the relative comfort of a tenure-track position in their country of birth. But consider the situation of immigrant faculty members who may depend on their jobs, not just for economic security, but as an escape from political persecution or instability (Barakat & Rodríguez, 2021).[10] And contingent faculty, whose positions and income are constantly shifting, uncertain, and poorly paid face a kind of double bind: because they are often traveling long distances to multiple low-paying jobs, they often do not have the time to write, to say nothing of the office space or institutional support needed to do so. Yet, if they don't write, they are unable to extract themselves from that situation.[11]

Another feature of the academic context that makes writing feel risky is the fact that it takes place within, not just a job market, but a "reputation market," in which a scholar's value and status are determined by their standing among their colleagues and advisors. In this reputation market, formal assessments of writing are rare and inconsistent, so graduate students and junior faculty members frequently find themselves unsure how to ask for and receive useful feedback from senior scholars. Then, when formal evaluations do take place, they are

> often attached to an abrupt and potentially career-altering decision: articles are accepted or rejected for publication, grant proposals are funded or denied, and job applications may be not only unsuccessful but even unacknowledged. When the evaluation is relatively rare, the possibility of rejection becomes more intimidating. (Houston, 2015, p. 76)

This combination—of long periods without feedback, peppered with occasional moments of high-stakes feedback—heightens the stakes of writing because they turn specific projects into proving grounds. That means the stress of evaluation is not just a general condition of the job. Instead, it's a stress that becomes concentrated on particular writing projects throughout the life of a scholar. So, for example, the literature review we discussed previously involves not just the inherent difficulties of writing. It's also what Houston refers to as a "ritual of evaluation," one that distills the risks to one's professional success down to one's performance on a particular writing project.

Within this unstable and uncertain structure of evaluation, scholars must rely heavily on impression management strategies to maintain their reputations with their peers and senior colleagues, constantly working to influence how they are perceived by others. This process of impression management begins at the first stages of the academic career, as Ferrales and Fine argue when graduate students

> must learn to recognize how each exchange with a faculty member has the potential to shape a student's budding professional reputation. Faculty assessments depend on several factors including students' presentation of self; the quality of the comments and questions posed in course discussions; the caliber of papers written during coursework; a student's publication record; obtaining outside recognition such as prestigious grants, fellowships, and awards; endorsements by other faculty members; and information gleaned from the graduate school application. (2005, p. 59)

In other words, scholars don't only need to successfully create high-quality research. We also need to actively manage more powerful scholars' awareness of our having done so by communicating and performing the quality of our thinking in the reputation market. And our success at doing so has significant impact. As Ferrales and Fine point out, "being told that one is a poor writer may discourage a student from continuing in school, considering the emphasis on publication as a necessity for career building. . . . Students come to define themselves in the eyes of others" (2005, p. 63).

What is particularly difficult about this process is that the working of this system is not made explicit, which means that scholars aren't always aware of the rules governing their interactions with those tasked with evaluating them. And "even when they do, they do not know how to play the game. Moreover, the uncertainty of not knowing one's standing in a cohort can be paralyzing to professional development" (Ferrales & Fine, 2005, p. 72). While they are talking about students, the same applies to junior faculty. We can think of graduate school and the tenure track as a boxing gym, in which competitors must learn how to make a fist, protect their bodies, and punch with power—all while in the middle of the fight. Now imagine that some competitors are taught these things, while others are not—they must pick up the skills by watching while amid the competition. This is what it's like for junior scholars who lack the mentoring and cultural capital to understand that they are not just studying a topic; rather, they are being socialized into a profession, and need to explicitly perform mastery if they want to thrive in the reputation market.

Nor does this work end once the degree is in hand, since junior faculty often have even fewer opportunities for evaluation. Instead, they may be broadly understood by their colleagues as having successfully passed through the formal apprenticeship period, and therefore no longer be in need of mentoring. At that point, criteria for evaluation become especially opaque. Standards for earning tenure are often implied, rather than expressly articulated, and they are very rarely written down. Thus, rather than operating with a clear sense of the standards against which they will be regularly and transparently evaluated, junior scholars operate in an environment where they are constantly managing others' impressions of them through words (written and spoken) and deeds.

To recap, job scarcity *changes the stakes* of writing by defining it as the mechanism by which we retain financial security. While the evaluation process *heightens the stakes* of writing, by converting specific writing projects into proving grounds that brook no error. What this means is that the projects that should be learning experiences, sites of innovation, and creativity for scholars of *all* ranks, instead become, as Houston refers to them, "rituals of evaluation," that amplify our anxiety and make us less willing to risk making mistakes.

A third feature of the academic professional context that makes writing risky is the way that social hierarchies change scholars' chances of successfully navigating the job and reputation markets mentioned earlier.[12] Social hierarchies are ranking systems that divide group members by social characteristics (e.g., race, gender, class, disability, immigration status, sexual preference, and gender expression). Scholars who are ranked higher in a social hierarchy receive more access to resources important to their success—for example, mentorship, training, and second chances—resources that in turn lead to greater opportunities for advancement in the profession. The reverse is true for scholars who are ranked lower on the social hierarchy: because of their lower status, they are subject to multiple forms of bias that make them more vulnerable to the job scarcity and evaluation process that mark academic life—even once they've earned tenure.

To see how this works, and how it can affect a scholar's writing, let's think back to the example of the literature review and how it might play out for different scholars. Dalia's program is in the US, and English is her second language. So she will be more likely to be judged harshly *for making the same errors* as someone who speaks English as their first language (Lindsey & Crusan, 2011). Or, consider the fact that as a woman, when Ana coauthors a manuscript, she will likely be seen as less qualified than Darnell if he does the same thing (Gërxhani et al., 2021). In her analysis of black women scholars' tenure denials, Patricia Matthew describes how social hierarchy impedes professional outcomes for women of color by interacting with the unspoken workings of the reputation market:

> While there certainly can be malice at work when faculty of color are assessed and evaluated, formally and informally, it is also the haphazard nature of these different processes that they are more structurally complicated for faculty of color than for their white counterparts. . . . I wouldn't try to argue that there was explicit bias. But what I've found is that there are codes and habits that faculty of color often don't know about because those unwritten practices are so subtle as to seem unimportant until something goes wrong, and then the assumption is that the person of color is incompetent, lazy, or lying. (Matthew, 2016, p. xv)

In an environment of economic uncertainty, hyper-competitiveness, uneven power, and lack of transparency, writing is far more than the work we engage in to communicate our ideas. Rather, writing is *also* the primary mechanism through which scholars establish security and a sense of personal worth in an ambiguous, unstable, uncertain, and unequal environment. We don't just write to convey what we know. We also (and at times primarily) write to bolster our reputation, prove our worth, counter racist and sexist assumptions, outshine our colleagues, and secure an increasingly finite set of resources. Graduate students write, not just to learn how to do a literature review, but to *prove* that they know how to do a literature review. Adjuncts, assistant professors, and postdocs write, present, and publish, not only because they want to join the conversation and share their work with the world, but because they are seeking to distinguish themselves in the job market.

Think, for example, of how you have made your own decisions about whether to accept an invitation to give a talk or present on a panel. What proportion of the time have you said yes merely because you enjoy the experience of sharing your work with a group of scholars from your field? And what proportion of the time has your mind leapt to how "good" the talk would look on your CV or how rare an opportunity it is to be able to establish a relationship with a leader in your discipline?[13] When writing is *also* the activity we engage in to establish and defend our professional identity and financial stability, it means the act itself becomes about other things because failing at that task can potentially weaken our chances of professional success.

These considerations are not shallow or inappropriate. They are necessary. And they illuminate the fact that while "the main task of academic writing is to *present* intellectual ideas, the *production* of academic writing is not solely an intellectual activity" (Antoniou & Moriarty, 2008, p. 160).

 ## Focus Point

Think about a time when one of the three risks of writing has affected your writing session. What did that look like? How did you respond?

Interpretive Challenges: The Impact of Risk on Writing

While these conditions are certainly challenging, they do not describe the steps by which we become stuck. As I've defined it in Chapter 1, "stuck" is more than the frustration of not knowing clearly what you mean to say or moving slowly in the production of the work. Scholars become stuck when we deliberately or unintentionally respond to that frustration in ways that are designed to shield us from the risks of writing rather than move us through them. You'll remember also that being stuck is not necessarily a permanent condition. Writers can get stuck selectively—that is, we can be stuck in one project while another moves merrily along. It's also possible to have long been a steady, productive, even happy writer; then to suddenly look up to find we're no longer the writer we once were. The question remains then: how do we get to the point where it's more important to protect ourselves from the risks of writing rather than take them?

The basic pattern I see most often among stuck scholars is that, when we encounter a challenge in our writing, we personalize instead of contextualize the problem. That is, rather than understand the challenge as endemic to writing (an aspect of Head, Hand, or Heart), or examine how the university setting makes the challenge especially difficult to manage, the stuck scholar will interpret *the challenge itself* as a function of their flawed character or limited ability. This happens even when we understand the pressures of academic life, or are adept at analyzing how context shapes and constrains the lives of community members that are part of our research. Instead, we lose the ability to understand the individual in context that comes so easily in our scholarship. As a result, we develop a limited view of why we are struggling with writing—one that names our incapacity as the primary explanation.

In addition to seeing ourselves as the source of our writing problems, scholars who are stuck in their writing often go one step beyond personalization to pathologize our challenges as somehow abnormal. We cast ourselves as suffering from flaws that are starkly deeper than or different from those of the rest of our cohort. Because the act of writing is often completed in solitude, it's easy to see how scholars can so easily lose perspective. In the words of one graduate student, "you're on your own, and it requires a great deal of diligence and discipline, and it's a lonely walk" (Fergie et al., 2011, p. 236). Without a community of support that reflects on your own experience, it's easy to rely instead on explanations of individual inadequacy (de Novais, 2018).

Scholars who are stuck often compare their performance to that of other (read: better, smarter, faster) imagined scholars, whom they believe have some secret knowledge of which they are unaware, something that eliminates that tortured process of writing and turns it into a smooth, even, unimpeded experience. Writing psychologists Flower and Hayes put it this way: "One of our subjects had just finished a writing session that looked like a wrestle with the devil; yet when we asked her to describe the normal process of a good writer, she replied that this mythical writer would 'just know exactly what she wants to say. She should just know what she wants to do . . . and *just write it*'" (Flower & Hayes, 2016, p. 32). Pathologizing is a crucial step on the road to being stuck because it is through pathologizing that writers shift from thinking of our *work* as the problem to thinking of *ourselves* as the problem. That is, we take our writing struggles as a sign that we are unworthy—that we're so inferior to our peers and senior colleagues that we're fundamentally incapable of the kind of thinking and communication that is the bread and butter of our profession. And therefore, we're "just not cut out" for academia.

Once a scholar becomes convinced that their writing problems are caused by unfixable personal flaws, it becomes easier and easier to manage the risk by avoiding the work completely. Pria isn't just worried about what her advisor will think—she's worried that he hasn't yet figured out that she's not smart enough to meet his expectations. So she Side Writes, day after day, with mounting frustration. Darnell, on the other hand, can't stand the discomfort of his messy, unclear thoughts on a page. He *knows* none of his colleagues can ever be as confused by their thinking. So he spends most of his writing time Not Writing so he can avoid having to face his weakness, day after day. This pattern is what psychologists refer to as the cycle of self-efficacy (Zumbrunn, 2021): First, we doubt our ability to do something. Then we avoid or engage minimally with the activity. Then because of that minimal engagement, we find that we're not as successful as we'd wanted to be. While it's useful to think about the habits of mind that lead to getting stuck, it's equally important to note that this pattern flourishes in exactly the conditions that are present in the academic reputation market and the social hierarchies that mark it: When we compare ourselves to others whose struggle we cannot see; when we receive negative feedback that's highly consequential; and when we experience the physiological responses that come with the stress of writing, we are much more likely to interpret ourselves as individually incapable (Zumbrunn, 2020, pp. 45–51). As education scholar, Janine de Novais explains in her poignant, trenchant analysis of her own experience of imposterism,

> I saw the experience of graduate school as one where I was often in close contact with the threat that I was flawed, unsuited for the task before me, and unworthy of being there. Shame and self-loathing were exacerbated in graduate school because, as a processual matter, graduate school connected my self-worth to my work. And then it proceeded to evaluate that work—and therefore evaluate me—relentlessly. (2018, p. 173)

This pattern of self-doubt can afflict any scholar. One common form it takes is the Imposter Phenomenon, in which high achievers feel unworthy of their successes despite significant and multiple achievements (Clance and Imes,

1978; Young, 2011). Perhaps you've felt it yourself—that terrible feeling that, despite the wealth of evidence to the contrary, you're not as competent or accomplished as other people seem to think you are, and therefore do not deserve and cannot trust your success (Clance & Imes, 1978). While researchers are divided over the gendered dimension of Imposterism (Bravata et al., 2020), the feeling is especially common among women as well as people of color, particularly in disciplines that treat "genius" as more significant than training (Muradoglu et al., 2021).

For scholars of color—or any marginalized groups—the pattern of pathologizing can take the specific form of stereotype threat, in which members of marginalized groups internalize negative stereotypes about themselves to the detriment of their performance. In her essay "The Making of a Token," Yolanda Flores Niemann provides a harrowing and insightful analysis of how stereotype threat changed her sense of professional competence. She explains how her colleagues' treatment transformed her from someone who had "strong feelings of self-efficacy in the academy to wondering why I had the arrogance to think I could succeed in an academic career" (2012, pp. 336–337).

A stunning piece that should be read in its entirety, Niemann's essay provides a powerful example of how Inherent and Institutional challenges can affect, not just a scholar's identity, but their practice of *writing* specifically. She explains that, as a result of a years-long experience of stigmatization and tokenism, she

> had begun to have difficulty focusing on my writing, something that had previously come easily to me. My lack of confidence had become such a problem that—in a couple of cases where editors had recommended that I revise and resubmit a manuscript—I convinced myself that the quality of my work was not good enough to rewrite. All of this was symptomatic of the effects of tokenism, stigmatization, racism, and stereotype threat. It was also an example of the way attributed ambiguity made me question whether I had ever deserved to be hired or published. Thus, my state of mind resulted from the negative attitudes and beliefs I had internalized as well as the behavior and attitudes of others. (2012, pp. 349–350)

Flores Niemann's analysis illustrates that scholars' personalization of their writing problems is not just a faulty individual response or a bad "mindset." Rather, getting stuck involves an interaction between the external environment of racialized risk and the internal interpretations she began to have of herself. Most importantly, Flores Niemann's piece shows how scholars who are stuck do not invent these interpretations out of thin air. Instead, the repeated instances of racial bias she encounters become the *ingredients* of her self-doubt. It's her negative experiences in the reputation market that make her question the worth of her ideas and eventually keep her from writing. Niemann's analysis also illuminates the close relationship between the act of writing and the development of our professional identity. It's not just that writing is the way we establish professional status and security. It's also the way we establish a sense of who we are as knowledge makers; it's the way scholars "make their findings known to the public and develop a sense of themselves as authorized scholars in their fields of practice" (Kamler & Thomson, 2008, p. 507). Feeling stuck then causes problems, not just for our ability to get our writing done. Feeling stuck often means we are also struggling with bigger questions about who we are and whether we even have the right to make certain intellectual claims.

The most significant impact of this pattern—of personalizing writing challenges—isn't its effect on writing productivity. As activist writing instructor Louise Dunlap points out (2007), the more meaningful aspect of this pattern is that it is a form of silencing. And it happens in at least two ways: One way is through the suppression of our ideas. In Flores Niemann's case, she lapsed into Not Writing—she merely stopped working on the manuscript, convinced that neither she nor it were good enough. We may also suppress our ideas through Side Writing. Take, for example, the activity of untamed literature searches, otherwise known as the Lit Review Rabbit Hole. When faced with an ill-formed, unproven idea they're unsure of, it's not unusual for scholars to look for reassurance by "double checking" to see if what anyone else has said affirms the idea. In essence, when we go down the Lit Review Rabbit Hole, we often ask ourselves "Am I allowed to say that?" and search for the answer in other people's thinking. In doing so, we are "checking in" to see if what we're saying is OK, instead of taking the risk of even speaking aloud to ourselves an idea that is half-formed and unconfirmed by others. This messy, risky work is exactly what we must be able to do to bring our nascent ideas to life. Yet, we are too fearful to do it when we are stuck.

Sarah Burton describes another example of this "double checking" pattern through which stuck scholars silence themselves. In her analysis of how women try to legitimize themselves and their work in the academic reputation market, she introduces us to Johanna, a working-class PhD student who describes her writing practice

in terms of shame and stigma—this included constant checks on aspects such as spelling and grammar, Johanna feeling that slipping on these parts of writing showed her as lacking the cultural or educational capital of her peers. To not use correct grammar or spelling would mark her out as unsophisticated, crude, and not grounded in high-quality prestigious education. (Burton, 2018)

What's important about both these examples is that they illustrate how Not Writing and Side Writing are more than the standard form of quality assurance in which every scholar must engage. Instead, these responses express scholars' fears and hesitations about how they will be perceived and interpreted in what they know is a classed and gendered reputation market. They experience these fears not abstractly, but in the moment of writing and so respond to them through the act of writing. As Dunlap puts it, "Most of us expect our writing to be criticized, so we protect ourselves by not writing what we mean. This is how silencing works: we develop our own internal judge. The blocks to freedom are right inside us" (2007, p. 32).

Another way we can silence ourselves—the one with which this book is most concerned—is by doubting or ignoring our writing process. One of the questions I receive most often from scholars is whether their writing strategy is "right" to use. Scholars will often lay out an involved process that they like to follow, one that makes sense to them given where they are in the manuscript and what they're struggling with: "I love to mind map," Georgia tells me, "I really can't make sense of things without it." Another retreater, Foster, explained to me that she had to make tables first, or else she couldn't even begin the data analysis paragraphs. When editing, Darnell and I are similar: there comes a point in writing when we can't move forward—*we actually can't see the argument we're making*—unless we print out the manuscript and lay it out on the floor. Time after time, scholars explain to me what makes sense in their heads, and what they have done in the past, with great animation and detail. After providing a description which, to me, is exactly what they need to do to write, they shyly ask, "Is that OK?"

When I ask scholars why it might *not* be OK for them to follow their process, their responses reveal how deeply silencing is connected to issues of trust. They say that they don't know if they're just "resisting" what they really need to be doing. Perhaps what they've just explained is just an elaborate Side Writing technique, they say. And besides, it takes such a long time—isn't there a faster way? These questions are fundamentally about whether they believe that what they are doing is the *real work* of writing, or whether it is a sneaky form of stuck. They do not trust themselves or their process. So, like Ana, who clings to an early morning writing schedule that doubles her work, they don't trust themselves to modify and experiment with their approach to writing.

Understanding stuckness as a form of silencing means that we have to recharacterize the problem: in other words, being stuck in our writing isn't just an intellectual or emotional problem; it's a power problem. One we face, not because we're trying to figure out our thoughts, but because we're trying to figure them out in order to gain or maintain a place in the scholarly community. And that struggle is made harder for some scholars than others because of the way universities reproduce social hierarchies. In addition, getting stuck is an understandable response to those conditions within which we work. As Feenstra et al. (2020) argue, getting stuck is not "a dysfunctional 'syndrome' that resides within certain individuals, but instead as a psychological response to a dysfunctional context."

Focus Point

To what extent have the risks of writing negatively impacted your ability to write? How have your responses mirrored or differed from those of the scholars described earlier in the chapter?

Is it any wonder, then, that we sometimes get stuck while writing? That the fits and starts of writing, no matter how natural they are, feel uncomfortable and at times, unbearable? Our ideas, when we first begin to play with them, are naturally ill-formed and uncertain; our prose is disjointed and ugly. Writing requires that we simultaneously expose and tolerate a level of ignorance and confusion that in general are devalued by our peers, whose bread and butter is the proffering and defense of elegant argument. Tolerating such discomfort, and muddling one's way through it without training in how to do so, is hard enough on its own. When experienced within the context of economic uncertainty, unequal treatment, and risk to our social and professional future, it is hardly surprising that we might turn away from writing and silence our most daring and interesting thoughts.

If you have been feeling alone and singular in your struggles with writing, I hope that this chapter has illustrated how untrue that is: you are not the only person who has faced and perhaps even felt beaten by these challenges. That is the first cause for hope: if you find yourself stuck, it's not because there's anything wrong with you. It's because writing *is ridiculously difficult,* even under the best, most supportive circumstances. And our responses to that difficulty are driven by physiology and profoundly conditioned by a professional environment that—rather than being supportive, often makes writing even harder than it already is. So writing becomes a risky endeavor, one so intimidating that it can cause us to so strongly internalize the voices of judgment that we silence ourselves.

Naming stuck as a power problem might seem to create an impossible additional hurdle for you to manage as a writer. I've laid out a scenario in which the structures that you're a part of might seem to bind you so much that either there is no hope at all or the only way to attack the problem is to fight the entire professional culture and structure of academia—which wouldn't help your writing in the least. But while you may be constrained by that environment, you are not predetermined by it. It is possible to navigate this treacherous territory. You've already done so, many, many times before. It's hard to remember, when the clock is ticking and imaginary reviewers sit, sneering, on your shoulder. But you already have an amazing resource at your fingertips that can help you get unstuck: you have your writing process. The steps you go through to get your ideas out of your head and onto the page. Your writing process is all yours. It's particular to you and has grown with you over time. And it makes writing not just less difficult but also more enjoyable, less lonely, and a truer expression of who you are as a writer and a thinker.

Let's give it a closer look.

Notes

1. Although descriptions of adjunct labor by Nzinga (2020) and others make clear that the working conditions of contingent faculty members are quite exploitative.

2. Writing is also a craft and Helen Sword talks extensively about that aspect (2017), while I focus here on the technical skill involved in learning the multiple genres that are part of academic writing.

3. Scholars who are neurodivergent must also contend with an added layer of disruption. Those diagnosed with Attention Deficit/Hyperactivity Disorder (ADHD), for example, may have trouble focusing on one idea for a long time or drawing from their working memory while crafting ideas (https://carleton.ca/determinants/2019/being-diagnosed-with-adult-adhd-as-a-professor/). These disruptions may be invisible, even to them—or if apparent, they may have the extra burden of feeling compelled to hide their condition from their colleagues.

4. See as well Paltridge, (2002), and Anderson et al., (2021), on the different types of dissertation.

5. Inadequacy when our committee tells us, once again, that more revisions are needed. Furious, frightened impotence when an editor or advisor insists, with no awareness, that we change the argument back to the one we'd been making nine months ago. Boredom when we think of having to write yet one more journal article.

6. As Wynne et al. (2014), show, scholars have slipped between using the term apprehension and anxiety. And as Rose (1984) and Hjortshoj (2001) both point out, scholars who are stuck aren't always anxious.

7. After writing this book, I now suspect that this is because the understanding of how to write a literature review is a form of tacit knowledge (see Chapter 3), one we pick up through doing rather than through explicit instruction. I can say for myself, that I only truly learned (rather than dimly perceived) the ins and outs of both literature reviews and ethnographic methods when I was forced to

teach these topics to undergraduates, and in the process of seeking clear definitions and explanations for what I wanted from them, found texts that finally explicitly conveyed what I'd been doing (and what I'd been doing incorrectly).

8. Thesen adopts Mary Louise Pratt's language of contact zones to describe the academic community, naming it as one of the many "social spaces in which cultures meet, clash and grapple with each other, often in contexts of highly asymmetrical relations of power, such as colonialism, slavery and their aftermaths" (quoted in Thesen & Cooper, 2014, p. 3).

9. As Usher suggests, we are now dealing with a knowledge economy that "replaces an epistemological with an economic definition of knowledge" (Usher, 2002, p. 44).

10. See especially the essays by Schoorman (2021) and Hardman (2021) in this same volume.

11. While I've been discussing faculty, the same situation applies to librarians as well: https://www.ala.org/advocacy/diversity/odlos-blog/laboring.

12. For a dazzling analysis of the impact of race and power in academic life, see Rockquemore and Laszloffy (2008).

13. And as Mountz et al. point out, the way we prove that worth is through counting. As universities do things like shorten the allowable time for the completion of the PhD, expect even more publications from new hires, and institute numeric assessment systems of scholarship, the meaning of writing changes so that "writing becomes an instrumental skill rather than an epistemological experience" (Mountz et al., 2015, 1241).

Turning Toward Yourself

How Writing Process Can Help You Get Unstuck

"The most beautiful thing we can experience is the mysterious. It is the source of all true art and science."

–Albert Einstein

It started with just a few extensions—small ones, really, just a day or two, so she could get the details just right. And her profs always gave them to her—she had a great reputation in her department as a sharp, kind, insightful student, someone who consistently submitted quality work. But by the end of her second year, Tiana was weighed down with two Incompletes and had to scramble to finish them up over the summer. Not long after, the pattern showed up in her projects as a Research Assistant.

She'd push off working on her section until the day before it was due to the research team. Then, panicked, she'd write in an exhausting frenzy 'til the work was what she considered "done." If it wasn't perfect by the time she'd agreed to share it, she just didn't send it off. No notice. No explanation. Just a growing sense of dread the entire time she worked to polish it. Every minute she was late was an additional degree of perfection she had to achieve. Every word she wrote was another wave of shame she had to endure. When she finally handed over the work, she was so beaten down that she couldn't bear the thought of writing again any time soon. And so, the cycle started all over again.

The worst part for Tiana was that she'd read the literature on writing productivity, and she *knew* what she was supposed to do. She *knew* she should follow Boice's advice and write regularly.[1] She even had a writing accountability group that met weekly—three other women who she liked, trusted, and had written with for several years. But still, the mere thought of opening her documents was unbearable. And even confessing her procrastination to her fellow writing group members couldn't induce her to work. Tiana had even read some of the work on the importance of slowing down the pace of academic work, but she hadn't seriously considered it—the mere idea just made her more anxious. What was even more confusing is that her struggle with writing wasn't even consistent: on some projects, she had no trouble getting started at all. On others, starting was nearly impossible. For yet a third category of projects, it wasn't starting that was difficult—it was stopping! It was maddening not knowing what the writing was going to be like that day. Which Tiana was she going to face when she sat down at her desk? And how could she ever trust herself to turn something in on time?

Tiana's dilemma is one that many scholars face when they turn to writing guides for help in getting unstuck. On the one hand, the literature on academic writing productivity provides crucial strategies for establishing a regular writing habit. It builds skills that are essential to intellectual work. And the scholars who've written on these topics have generated an essential change in the profession: they've made conversations about writing public and common, while clarifying some of the key routes to regular writing. But as we saw in the previous chapter, problems like Tiana's involve more than showing up to the desk. They involve wading through the feelings that appear once they've arrived: not just the feelings of worry or insecurity, but more importantly, the sense that they lack authority—that they have no *right* to say what they think and may never gain access to their scholarly community. To handle those challenges to confidence and authority, we often lean heavily on discipline, force, and external motivators to push us through the difficult times. Unfortunately, confidence and authority problems do not respond well to discipline and force.

One powerful but overlooked strategy for developing a confident sense of authority in your writing is to uncover and use your unique writing process to overcome writing challenges. Each of us—whether we think consciously about it or not—has an approach to writing that just feels more natural. It makes more sense. It's just "how we do things." We might not know all the pieces of this process. But there are bits of it that, when we follow them, help us manage the moments when we are too unsure of our own capacity or authority to move forward. Following your unique process will not magically make writing a breezy, carefree walk in the park. But it *can* improve your ability to think clearly and problem-solve in the face of overwhelm, anxiety, and self-doubt.

How does that happen? Chapters 4 and 5 will help you explore and expand your own unique writing process. Before we do that, however, we'll take the time in this chapter to more fully explore what a writing process is. First, we'll expand the initial definition you found in Chapter 1 and explore why process receives so little attention from scholars. Then we'll look at a model of writing process that describes the key moments we move through when creating a manuscript. Next, we get concrete, as I give examples of what writing process looks like for real scholars. Finally, we'll examine how understanding process can help you manage Inherent, Institutional, and Interpretive writing challenges.

What Is Writing Process?

As I mentioned in Chapter 1, writing process is, quite simply, the series of steps we take to move from the initial, muddy thinking in our heads to the clear, well-crafted assembling of words on the page. We generally think of these steps, if we think of them at all, as including the things we do to clarify our ideas: the drafting, composing, deleting, and revising we do to get that idea *just* right. While all of those steps are indeed a part of your writing process, they only comprise part of writing: its *cognitive* and *technical* components. This includes all of the thinking work we do to understand what we want to say and the structure (or genre), we will use to say it. However, as Chapter 2 illustrated, writing also has an *emotional* dimension—it's a process awash in feeling, both about the ideas that we work with and the way we express and share them. In addition, writing has a *sociopolitical* dimension. We write, not merely to please ourselves, or clarify our thinking to ourselves and others, but also to secure our place in an intellectual and professional community that assesses what we do. This means that writing, which seems on the surface like a simple, solitary act, is actually a complex set of relational activities, in which we're interacting symbolically, virtually, and actually with other scholars.

Our writing process, therefore, includes all the steps we take to make our way through the cognitive, technical, emotional, and political dimensions of a writing project. Writing process is not magical—understanding one's own will not suddenly and automatically eliminate the difficulties of writing. Nor does recognizing the value of your own writing process make you precious—it won't become impossible for you to write if you're unable to meet a finicky set of conditions. Process is not some mercurial and exacting muse without which the writer cannot move forward. But following your process *will* make your writing session easier, more efficient, and more pleasurable. If, for example, your ideas flow more easily when you first outline them on note cards, you will not be incapacitated if you run out of cards. You may find however, that it takes a little longer to get in the flow of writing or see the relationship between concepts.

Similarly, writing process is not a set of activities designed to "inspire" a scholar to write. While going through your process can certainly boost your desire to write or remind you of why you're so enthusiastic about this topic in the first place, its primary purpose is not to make a scholar *want* to sit down and write. Rather, its purpose is to help you begin or stick with writing, even when you don't feel like it. It does so by providing a familiar, well-worn path through the thicket of thoughts and feelings that can stand in your way.

Given how central writing is to scholars' work and success, it's something of a mystery that our profession has so little to say about it. Regardless of whether you are a first-year graduate student, or a full professor at a research one university, you are, essentially, a professional writer. Not only are you constantly producing reports, class lectures, and public talks, but the publication and funding that are the most coveted rewards of our profession are achieved primarily through writing. Without a clear understanding of our own particular writing process, even accomplished academics with a disciplined daily writing practice can be easily disrupted: the time we do spend writing can be less fruitful and therefore more frustrating; and like Tiana, our work process may restrict, rather than cultivate, the creativity and imagination required to develop and communicate our ideas. More abstractly, but perhaps most importantly, when we engage in our work in an unthinking manner, we lose the opportunity to enjoy its pleasures and beauty. The small moments of satisfaction that make all the effort worth it and keep us dedicated to the work even when the going gets tough.

And yet, there is a logic to our profession's blind spot, even if it doesn't appear to make sense. One reason why scholars do not think more systematically about writing may be that it is somewhat of a mystery. Einstein tells us, in the opening epigraph, that this mystery is the root of the work that we do as scholars—regardless of our discipline. But scholars do not cotton to the uncontrolled nature of the writing mystery. Writing is an unruly creative process that is nearly impossible to standardize. As Antoniou and Moriarty point out, academics prefer to maintain a false division between creative and academic work, a division that is a "relic of Western Enlightenment thought, which unfortunately persists in the twenty-first-century university. Rationality, intellect, and logic—the 'academic'—are reified, whilst imagination, emotion, and physical and natural rhythms—the 'creative'— are denigrated" (2008, p. 159). Scholars often don't want to think of the work we do as creative because we conflate creative work with work in an imaginary world, or at least one that is highly symbolic rather than based in evidence-based claims-making. Part of the assumption here is that creative work is false because it makes something out of nothing. Fiction writers and poets, for example, are creative writers, because they are "inventing" stories that are based on nothing other than their own imaginations.

However, this is a limited understanding of creativity, which is more accurately understood as the ability to form something new, often through the unexpected combination of existing material. Creativity is *exactly* the job of scholars. Contributing something "new" to our respective literatures is one of the basic requirements of any piece of scholarship. That requires our ability to develop new ways of thinking, new ideas, and new combinations. In other words, scholarship is built on creativity, imagination, and innovation.

Yet even those of us who reject this false division may wish, in our hearts, that writing was more manageable. More cut and dried and predictable— something easier to plot out on a calendar. While this chapter will show that researchers have mapped the stages of the writing process, the way any of us move through these stages varies from person to person, making it impossible to identify one "best" way to writing productivity.

Another reason that scholars do not think about writing may be that we very rarely *identify* as writers. That is, as a group, we do not typically see writing as central to our professional identity. Consider, for example, how you and your colleagues respond when asked what you do for a living: most mention that you are instructors, scholars, or researchers; very few identify ourselves as writers, even though writing is so central to what we do. I still remember the moment when a friend introduced me to a writer, claiming "Michelle's a writer too!" "Really!" said the stranger, with high-pitched delight. It was years after having published and received recognition for academic and creative work, in written and audio form—and still, I found myself hesitant to confirm my friend's clearly overblown characterization. "Only academic stuff," I muttered and began peppering her with questions to take the focus off of me.[2]

To the extent that academics *do* think about writing process, we often focus our attention on what it's like when we are *not* writing. While it's certainly useful to understand how to manage the moments when words do not come, our emphasis on being blocked limits our ability to create a writing process that works for us. It's as if someone has asked us how we get from home to work each day, and instead of describing our regular route, we delineate the headaches of what happens when there's a major traffic jam or a delay because of the weather. While that information is handy in an emergency, it doesn't help us determine the most efficient and beautiful route to work. What happens when we take the side streets? If we drive at 30 mph the entire way, can we hit all green lights? Our ability to write consistently, productively, and joyfully depends on our awareness of what our habits are, and which work best for unlocking our thinking. Yet because academics think of writing as a problem to be endured rather than a puzzle to be solved, we do not spend as much time as we should considering that question. So let's take a different approach: let's lay out the pieces of the writing process puzzle, see what they reveal, and what we can learn from them.

FIGURE 3.1 ● The Writing Process

Stages of the Writing Process

While the particular steps a scholar goes through are all their own, we all proceed through a common set of stages when generating our work. The model I describe here draws on multiple sources (especially Bane, 2012; Evans, 2013) and consists of seven stages, each of which has distinct features and challenges. While it would be wonderful to proceed through these stages in an easy, unbroken line, the fact is we weave in and out of most of the stages many times over the course of a project.

Initiation

The first stage of the writing process is Initiation, when we come upon an idea about what to write. It often takes place when we come across something that raises a question we find interesting. A student asks a question in class. We hear something on the news or in a conversation that makes us wonder if anyone's ever actually studied that. Or someone makes an assertion we *know* is baseless—and spurs our attempts to prove them wrong. Initiation can also be required by others—as is the case when graduate students are asked to write a seminar paper for a class. And it can be *inspired* by others, as is often the case when we read a Call for Submissions or the description of a conference theme.

We often think that ideas come to us in response to one single prompt. Yet cognitive psychologists who study writing point out that our ideas about what we want to say are deeply connected to the multiple boundaries that surround a project—what they refer to as "constraint." The writing that we do

> starts not with a single idea or intention, but with a set of external and internal constraints. These are some combination of a given task or assignment (such as the title for a college essay), a collection of resources (for example tables of data . . .), and the physical and social setting in which the writer is working (such as in front of a word processor in . . . an office, or holding a pen and staring at a blank sheet of paper in a class-room), and aspects of the writer's knowledge and experience including knowledge of language and the writing topic. (Sharples, 1999, p. 6)

It's tempting to dismiss the constraint introduced by course assignments as somehow inferior to those moments when ideas come from our own personal or intellectual interests. However, Sharples's comment illustrates that an assigned writing task is not distinguished by the existence of constraint. Rather, all instances of writing are marked by constraint. In fact, the limitations we experience are helpful for "focusing the writer's attention and channeling mental resources" (Sharples, 1999, p. 6).[3]

Saturation

The second stage of writing is referred to as Saturation. This takes place when we bring together and immerse ourselves in large quantities of information to help us better understand our topic. And it lasts until the writer is unable to (1) take in any more information or (2) make any more progress. The primary purpose of Saturation is for the scholar to increase their understanding of what has already been said on the topic at hand and to clarify what they would like to add to what already exists.

Saturation includes formal and structured forms of analysis that are taught by our disciplines and interdisciplines, such as observation, surveys, reading, formula construction, interviewing, and archival work. It can also involve less formal strategies of assembling and considering information on our topic: paying attention to things you see in popular culture and the news; making notes and gathering sources; and attending talks related to your subject. When in the moment of Saturation, the scholar has a heightened sense of awareness of a topic and is focused on bringing together a large number of related ideas and sources. Many of these ideas will eventually be eliminated, but all are up for consideration at the moment. "I'm just kind of . . . creating a stew," is how scholar Chris Watkins describes it. "Putting things together, trying out phrases, talking with people, letting it waltz all around" (Carnell et al., 2008, p. 36).[4]

Watkins's description of his writing vividly illustrates Laurel Richardson's point that writing and research are not distinct processes and that "writing is not just a mopping-up activity at the end of a research project" (1994, p. 516). Instead, while taking in everything we can about the topic, we are simultaneously trying to understand, connect, organize, and articulate our own and others' ideas. Therefore, writing (the process of communicating one's ideas in written form) and research (the process of generating, investigating, developing, and verifying arguments) often happen at the same time. And according to some scholars, *should* happen at the same time, to improve the quality of the final piece of scholarship (Janesick, 2011).

Incubation and Illumination

The third stage of the writing process takes place when a writer ceases active, purposeful consideration of ideas and allows the unconscious mind to continue to work on a puzzle or topic without his deliberate awareness and action. We often find ourselves in this phase when we come to an impasse—when the trail of ideas we were following runs out—and deliberate thinking about the problem no longer yields the results we were looking for.

In my observation, Incubation is many scholars' least favorite stage of writing, because it's the moment that's least likely to generate tangible, visible evidence of work. In other words, Incubation often looks and feels as though you're not doing anything at all—as though, in fact, you are slacking off from work and instead engaged in leisure activity. To Incubate is to take a shower, or a walk. To practice piano scales or free throws. To weed the garden. In other words, Incubation is happening when our conscious attention is focused on something other than our manuscript. And Incubation is the phase least under our control and therefore least responsive to overwork. We can cobble together a passable substitute for what we really mean to say, papering the holes in our argument with omission and obfuscation. But no amount of pushing will speed along the process of making an unconscious connection. You have to cultivate conditions that make creativity happen, not push it. Incubation is not only important to our ability to develop our ideas, solve puzzles, and come up with new ideas. It is often an actual requirement of moments of the fourth stage of writing—Illumination (Kounios & Beeman, 2015). These are the "Aha" moments during which ideas and solutions appear to us, seemingly like magic.

Clarification

Clarification is the most sought-after and misunderstood of all the moments of writing. During Clarification, writers are "devoting full mental resources to transforming a chain of associated ideas into written text" (Sharples, 1999, p. 7). Clarification is the most visibly productive stage of the writing process, because it leads to additional words, or at the least, changes in the order of words and the writer's understanding of them. Those who discuss writer's block tend to describe Clarification as the first moment in which words and ideas are being produced by the writer. Roseanne Bane describes this moment as the one when we "transform the insight and passion of the Illumination into something tangible that can be shared with others" (Bane, 2012, p. 77). While Kate Evans refers to this moment as "Engagement" and sees it much like a moment of flow, in which "we are stoked and rolling. We are in a comfortable rhythm, the words are presenting themselves easily" (2013, p. 17). This conception of Clarification is represented by the concept, familiar to any who is ABD,[5] of "writing up." This idea suggests that generating sentences and paragraphs is something we only do after research, reading, and thinking are complete. It's as though composition were "an add-on to research and scholarship instead of an integral part of it. It's as if 'writing-up' were a separate coda to the main research opus" (Badley, 2009, p. 209).

There are two problems with this conceptualization of Clarification. The first is that it's inaccurate. Whether we appreciate them or not, the things we do before Clarification are all essential elements of writing. The second problem with this conceptualization of Clarification is that it devalues the work that's essential to composition. I cannot count the number of scholars I've talked with who, when describing a mountain of reading, note-taking, and clarifying, will minimize their efforts by saying that it wasn't "real" writing, and feel genuine and deep-seated frustration that they "didn't get anything done." Labeling the previous stages of writing as insignificant is akin to saying that the only time scholars spend on teaching is when they're in the classroom in front of their students. While the time spent searching the literature, picking materials, building a syllabus, and creating lectures and lesson plans is not "real."

And yet there is something different happening in this stage, isn't there? There is something about the process of finally fitting together a mass of words so that they fit neatly into each other like puzzle pieces. It is more visible than other phases of writing, it feels more tangible. It's important to be clear about what those differences are—not to quibble over definitions, but because when we are clear about what's actually happening in this stage, we are clearer about the pitfalls we face and ways to get past them.

What distinguishes Clarification from the other stages of the writing process is not that it's the first moment that we're "writing," but that it's the first moment that we're primarily writing for others. We therefore make three shifts during Clarification that distinguish it from other stages of the writing process. The first is a shift in audience. In all the stages before Clarification, we, the writer, are our primary audience. That doesn't mean we don't share our ideas with others, or even samples of what we have written down in these first three phases. It doesn't mean that we aren't thinking of others sometimes. It just means that the reader's job, to the extent that she is present, is to help us talk to ourselves. We might think of others, if we are being blunt, as a prop—as an acting partner who helps us run our lines. They are important only as an interlocutor who helps us improve our performance. Once we move into Clarification, however, our imagined reader becomes our audience. We have a better sense of what we mean, and while some internal Clarification must take place, we now are devoted to speaking directly and deliberately to our external reader.

The second characteristic that distinguishes Clarification from the previous stages of writing is a shift in its purpose. Before Clarification, we aim to uncover our thinking. How are we defining this term? What did we mean when we wrote that phrase? What do we know for certain about this relationship or another? We do not come to our research project with our ideas fully formed—we have slivers of ideas, scraps—which we develop in conversation with other scholars, and which must be clarified before we can share them with others. In Clarification, however, our purpose shifts from *discovering* our own thinking for ourselves to *explaining* our thoughts to others. Clarification is the moment when we take all the pieces that we have and try to put them together in a way that makes sense for an external reader. To say it in a way they find clear, persuasive—and if you love wordplay—elegant.

Finally, because our audience and purpose shifts during Clarification, so too does the format of our writing. In the first three or four stages of our process, writing can be in any format—as long as it accomplishes the goal of helping us uncover our thoughts for ourselves. It works whether it is in paragraphs or the shorthand form of notes, charts, graphs, formulas, maps, outlines, or images. All of these forms are meant to capture the essence of ideas for us, for our current and future use. Even if they are in paragraphs, the paragraphs may have a tone and style that doesn't match the one we eventually take in this phase. We do not need, in the early stages, to follow formal rules of grammar and style, except to the extent that those rules help us make sense of our own thinking. Even when we share work with others, we can pass along our scribblings with the injunction that the reader "ignore all my typos" and just comment on the essence of the idea.

However, as we attempt, in Clarification, to order and explain our thoughts as much as possible for others, these more shorthand forms are converted into paragraphs, the reigning queens of the scholarly writing universe. The paragraphs are arranged into the section and order that is standard for our field. If visual or shorthand representations of our ideas remain on the page, these methods of capturing information are typically relegated to the status of "visual aid." It is this *combined* shift in audience, purpose, and format that makes Clarification different from other stages of the writing process—not the fact that writing is happening for the first time. At this point, we aim to create as cogent an argument as possible for the reader who lives outside our minds.[6]

Submission

While not mentioned in most models of writing and creative process, my experience as a coach, scholar, and writer has shown me that there is a sixth stage that is particularly important for scholars: Submission. This is the moment when you share what you've written with others, taking the conversation out of your head and into a live dialogue. Submission is a deliberate act of letting go of your writing, even if temporarily and prematurely, in a way that allows you to further refine it. Because it involves interaction with and feedback from others, it often initiates a phase of winnowing, refinement, and even defense of our ideas. Thus, while we think of it as something that takes place *after* we write, Submission is no less a moment or act of development of your thinking than checking a citation or drawing on a theoretical framework.[7]

Submission isn't just the moment when you present at a conference or publish a manuscript, although, of course, those are the moments that are most highly recognized and rewarded by the profession. It's also happening when you share an outline with a colleague; submit a chapter to your dissertation committee; even when the dean asks, "So what do you work on?" at the college's fall reception. When you give a guest lecture to undergraduates that draws from your research; when you ask your colleague two doors down to listen to your ideas and make sure they make sense. All of these are moments of Submission, because you are sharing your ideas about your work.

Submission is essential to the forward movement of your writing, because it's the moment when you get feedback that makes your ideas better. Sharing our work with our community and audience is the ultimate purpose of our writing. Without Submission, there is really no point in writing a manuscript. Yet, as true as that may be, Submission is still a particularly risky moment in the writing process, since it exposes you to criticism that can help or hinder your work, depending on how it's delivered. While we may feel many fears while engaged in the previous stages of the writing process and imagine our audience in a way that causes anxiety, Submission is a moment of *actual* exposure to the judgments that are often at the heart of being stuck in writing. As such, it's worth highlighting this moment in the process.

In fact, Submission is the moment that stuck scholars are often most keenly aware of even when it's far off. It is the moment we are dreaming of, pining for, and writing toward. It causes significant anxiety for many of us, yet it's also a highly valuable, underappreciated, and underutilized opportunity for the development of our thinking—and thus deserves significant attention in any model of the writing process.

Hibernation

There you are. You've put the finishing touches on your manuscript. You pressed send, or deposited, or presented—you are truly finished. This is the moment we've all been waiting for, the moment we've been straining toward and dreaming of all this time. Think of all the times you worked yourself like a dog and still felt only frustration because the manuscript wasn't done. The hot shame you felt when someone asked how the dissertation was going. The times with kids and friends and beloved ones you gave up or minimized in order to reach this moment.

You've waited so long and worked so hard to get here. And yet, the moment we all dream of is the most fleeting and gossamer of all. Many scholars spend very little time in conscious acknowledgment and celebration of the moment when we finish. Instead, we tend to do one of two things: We collapse into exhaustion. Or we look up at the pile of manuscripts waiting for our attention and dive into the next one. Neither response is ideal if you're concerned about your well-being as a human and a writer. Each of these reactions skips the final phase of the writing process, the one that's perhaps most important for maintaining a long-term writing practice.

The final moment of the writing process is Hibernation. At this point in the writing process, the work is finished. The argument is as complete as it is going to be. The manuscript has been copyedited and submitted. Even though the publication may be only one part of a multi-manuscript project, this phase of that project is complete, and you're not actively engaged in further developing the idea within that particular manuscript. While Submission is universally engaged in but typically unrecognized, Hibernation is vaguely recognized and almost universally ignored. To the extent that the value of rest is acknowledged by many scholars, it is publicly devalued and those who engage in it may be shamed (Fitzgerald, 2015). Yet despite this attitude toward Hibernation, there is a wealth of research that shows us, unequivocally, that the Hibernation period is essential to the ability to maintain a sustained and sustainable writing practice and to spend that practice generating interesting and original ideas (Pang, 2016).

Hibernation looks a lot like Incubation, as both involve the deliberate retreat from active intellectual work. But Incubation's ultimate purpose is progress, forward movement. It aims to find a solution to an organizational, expressive, or intellectual dilemma presented by the manuscript by relying on the brain's power of unconscious association. Hibernation, on the other hand, is not meant to move work forward in any manner. Its sole purpose is to restore the energy and enthusiasm that is inevitably used up by long-term research and writing projects and the final push required to get them out the door.

While Hibernation involves a pause in work, it is not a vacation—the emphasis during vacations is on leisure or recreation.[8] Instead, writers Hibernate to conserve our few remaining resources and restore our depleted energy. We are like the plants and animals that face a long winter in which food is scarce. Like them, writers who have just finished a project often find that we're tapped out once we've submitted a manuscript and may be facing an extended period without energy, enthusiasm, or motivation for work. We may be jubilant about the project's end, perhaps even eager to move on to a long-delayed and more exciting project. But we also may find that attention and energy are hard to come by. The extra juice we need to keep going feels harder to access. To Hibernate is to purposefully allow your writing life to lie dormant, to exert as little effort as possible to keep things running, so you can build your energy back up and be ready for the moment when there's more to feed you.

What Writing Process Looks Like

This model of the writing process is helpful in at least two ways. The first is that it illustrates the contention, long held by coaches and dismissed by scholars, that writing includes more than composition. This insistence on such a narrow definition of writing is one of the primary causes of suffering among scholars. Wedded to the idea that the only real work to be done is the creation of new prose, we will often feel dejected and demoralized when we are in phases of manuscript production that do not generate new words or high word count. Yet, this model illustrates that clinging to such a narrow definition of writing is folly.

The other advantage of working with a model of the writing process is that it helps us identify what stage of writing we're in and what the primary focus of our work should be. Even the most cursory exposure to the model gives guidance about what scholars should and should not expect to see depending on where we are in the process. If you are in Initiation, for example, there's no reason to expect that you'd be creating reams of well-thought-out, cogent, and well-defended arguments. Instead, your focus is snatches of ideas, even if they make no sense.

The best way to fully understand the writing process is to consider a concrete example. Camila is a fourth year, tenure-track faculty member in Philosophy, who lives quite far from campus—nearly 2.5 hours away by public transportation. When they begin work on a section or chapter, they start by getting up slowly. They like to wake up and lie in bed and randomly think about their manuscript and the rest of the day ahead. They walk the dog and have coffee and some breakfast. Then they make contact with the outside world by spending about fifteen minutes checking Twitter. Throughout this morning routine, Camila is vaguely thinking about their manuscript. Not in an intense way, but thoughts are drifting into their head. They're in the Initiation stage, turning over ideas for a new section in their mind before they get to their desk. Before they officially get started, they'll write down a couple of bullets about what they're going to get done that day.

Camila works in two different locations: their home and cafes. When they start, the first thing they do is read. Ideally, for at least an hour. They're moving slowly into Saturation and think of this time as "intellectual play." It's as if they're in a tot lot, just messing around with beautiful ideas. It's fun for them to read what people are thinking, to think about how it fits with what they want to say. Their reading typically produces an epigraph they use to start their chapter or section. Not only does the epigraph remind them of the work they've read, but it also represents the central organizing idea of the section they're working on—a device that helps them start the writing. After about an hour of reading, Camila is ready to move to the next phase of writing: play on the page.

At this point, Camila handwrites the ideas they're thinking about on a separate sheet of paper with a pen. It's not important what form the writing comes in here. Often, it's bullets, but it can be sentences and paragraphs depending on where they are with their thinking. They're in the Initiation stage, determining whether what they thought the hour before makes sense once it's on the page. What's most important for Camila at this point is that they work in a medium that signals to them that, while they are trying to bring order to their words, they are not yet in the "serious" stage of writing. No one is going to read this work unless they invite them to, which they never would. Nothing here has to be orderly or sensical. All that's happening is that Camila is trying to bring some form to the ideas that emerged in their intellectual playground so that they are made "better"—a designation that even now, Camila has trouble characterizing. They just know "better" when they see it.

At some point, the ideas they're working on start coming faster than their pen can keep up with. They might not know exactly where they're going to land with everything, but they have a pretty good idea of where they're going. At this point, Camila is ready to move to the computer, where they start putting their ideas in some kind of order using Scrivener. They can't move to this platform too early. If they do, then the writing feels "meaningful." They get nervous if their thoughts aren't clear and at least partially ordered. So they wait until the right moment to move here. But inevitably, because of the nature of writing—they'll hit a point where the work isn't flowing as well.

This is the moment when it's easy for Camila to get stumped. Because they're a junior faculty member, and a high-achieving, driven person, any delay in their work feels pressing for them. Their tenure case is not threatened, but Camila so wants to get their work done quickly that the delays in writing typically cause a cascade of doubts to flood their mind. They chastise themselves for moving so slowly; they wonder if the book is ever going to get done. They begin imagining the encounters they'll have in the hall when they see their colleagues, and they ask how the book is going. These mental loops tend to occur when Camila is tired. They also occur when they're dealing with something theoretically challenging. They're not in Incubation yet; they keep banging away at the problem for several minutes more until they finally wear themselves out. Finally, in desperation, and because their dog is now giving them that look, they take a break. They make a cup of tea. Take the dog on a walk. Maybe get back on Twitter for a while (Incubation). If they're lucky, a small possibility occurs to them. Something they *just might* be able to use (Illumination). They dash off a few quick notes about a possible solution (Initiation), clear enough so they can pick it up the next day and see whether the idea might work (Clarification).

Camila's example illustrates several interesting features of the writing process and how it works. The first is that Camila moves in and out of several phases of the writing process in just one day of writing—and they don't even go "in order." While they begin in the Saturation phase, musing over the ideas in the reading, they move eventually to the Initiation phase, where they capture their own thinking on what they've read, in note form. Then they move to Clarification until they hit a stopping point and muscle through Incubation and Illumination.

Second, Camila's process, like all of ours, has a cognitive, technical, and emotional dimension to it: their cognitive work begins even before they're "officially" working, and it takes place in locations (walking the dog, while on Twitter) that we would not normally associate with writing. We also see just one of the many unique methods they have for handling the technical work of writing—their use of an epigraph as an organizing theme of a chapter or section. Finally, we can see very clearly the emotional dimensions of Camila's process. Like all of us, they sometimes get derailed by the intellectual conundrums raised by the writing process and respond by recalling the risks they're facing (exposing their ideas) which raises their level of anxiety (they won't finish the book in time). The context in which they operate includes the chorus of people they imagine commenting judgmentally on the speed of their writing once they see them in the hallway.

A third thing to note about Camila's process is that despite the fact that they are a regular, productive writer, they do not follow all of the best practices recommended in the literature. For example, Camila does not schedule their writing, as they do not keep a calendar, except to note special meetings. They have a very routinized schedule, partly because they live so far away from campus. With a 2.5-hour public transportation commute, it's clear every day when they have to leave and what time they have to get up to do so. They know exactly how much time they have to write. They prep for class on the train, and any prep that doesn't get done, they just drop. They also begin their writing day by surfing social media—a behavior that any coach would warn against.[9] Yet for Camila, this routine draws them toward their writing, rather than pulling them away in distraction. Camila illustrates the findings of recent scholars that not everyone's process needs to follow supposed "best practices" to be effective.

Finally, and most importantly, Camila's behavior illustrates that writing process isn't just a way for us to record information. Instead, writing process is how we make sense, meaning, and beauty of our thoughts. In Camila's case, they do not merely follow a set of neutral, universal steps that increase productivity. Rather they use their scrolling, reading, handwriting, typing, and epigraphs to enjoy and make sense of the material with which they are working.

Using Process to Get Unstuck

Following your writing process and attending to all of its dimensions can help you get unstuck in three different ways. First, it clarifies what conditions support, rather than squelch, your ability to write. When we uncover our writing process, we better understand the significance of what we do. For example, it was only after analyzing their process that Camila was able to recognize that moving from pen and paper to Scrivener heightened the stakes of writing for them and increased their anxiety unless they felt fully prepared. There's nothing in public conversations about the writing process that might have led them to believe that this mattered. Nor is there anything about working on the computer that necessarily leads scholars to give more weight to their words. But *for Camila*, this step has crucial, personal meaning—for no reason that either of us could ever discern. Frankly, the whys and wherefores do not matter. What matters is that Camila understands the emotional significance of working in one medium versus another. They, therefore, adjust their behavior accordingly, to make sure they are emotionally *and* intellectually ready for whatever platform they're in. In short, knowing what conditions support your writing makes it easier to avoid the difficult and derailing emotions inherent to the act. It also makes it easier to manage them when they do arise.

With one small move, Camila was able to enhance the degree of comfort and confidence they feel when writing. This illustrates a second way that understanding your process can help you get unstuck: as it did with Camila, being clear about your process can strengthen your sense of authority as a writer and scholar. One of the most common patterns I see as a writing coach is that scholars are relatively comfortable with their writing process before attending graduate school. But once they arrive, they begin to judge it (as simplistic, juvenile, inefficient, etc.) or to receive advice from trusted advisors and colleagues that contradicts what they have done in the past. Understandably eager to learn from those with more experience or facing a new problem they can't seem to solve on their own, scholars will let core elements of their writing process lapse, even after they find that new techniques do not serve them. But exploring and following your process—even when it does not match the advice of research or advisors—is one way that you can take ownership of your writing practice.

Not only can the writing process model help us clarify what's happening with our own writing. It can also help disrupt our tendency to misinterpret other scholars as people who have no trouble with writing at all. Take, for example, Noam Chomsky, who writes that

> I almost never work from an outline or follow a plan. The books simply grow by accretion. The reason for the twenty-minute spurts—which is a bit of an exaggeration; maybe hour spurts would be more accurate—is just the nature of my life, which happens to be very intense. I have two full-time professional careers, each of them quite demanding . . . and that doesn't leave much time . . . I discovered over the years that probably my only talent is this odd talent I seem to have that other colleagues don't, and that is that I've got sort of buffers in the brain that allow me to shift back and forth from one project to the other and store one. I can pick up after a long stretch and be more or less where I left off. (Olson, Faigley, & Chomsky, 1991, p. 4)

This depiction of the writing process is maddening. For those of us who struggle to find time, stay focused, and produce even a few lines of decent prose, it's hard not to be both jealous and suspicious of the idea of a book magically "growing" in this manner. The impression one gets is that he just sits down at his desk, prepared for the phase of Clarification, and ideas just roll off of his fingers onto the page.

However, once we hear Chomsky talk in more detail about exactly the various phases of his process, we can see that his manuscripts don't just "grow" on their own. For example, he also says that

> I don't recall ever having sat down and planned a book—except maybe for saying, 'Well, I'm going to talk about X, Y, and Z, and I'll have Chapter One on X, Chapter Two on Y, and Chapter Three on Z.' Then it's just a matter of getting the first paragraph, and it just goes on from there . . . it's probably because I've thought about most of it before, or lectured on it before, or written a letter to someone about it, or done it twenty times in the past. Then it becomes mainly a problem of trying to fit it all in. (Olson, Faigley, & Chomsky, 1991, p. 5)

These comments make clear that the progress Chomsky makes in the Clarification stage is the result of a long process of repeated Clarification and Submission. For weeks, if not months or years, he writes on a topic and shares it in formal and informal, written and verbal form. And while he may not present these ideas as a book—may not even be thinking of them as a book—he is working through his ideas so thoroughly that once he reaches Initiation ("Hmmmm, look at everything I've written about that—is that a book?"), he has been through the remainder of the stages so many times that the book seems to, as he says "go on from there."

To write is to navigate life. Writing challenges our confidence, exposes our insecurities, and demands our best self. It gives us many opportunities each day to sit down and be who we want to be or to be someone by whom we are frustrated and disappointed. How are we going to go through the challenges of writing? As an underling concerned with winning their advisor's approval? Or as a scholar who takes risks and experiments to find what works for them? How are we going to respond to the task of showing our understanding of existing research? As a defensive gesture to prove that we know our stuff? Or as the basis for intellectual growth that contributes to the communities that matter most to us? When we sit down to write each day, we meet the fears that come when we realize that our job is to know what we don't yet know. Understanding our writing process makes meeting those fears just a little bit easier, and a little bit more satisfying.

And this sense of satisfaction is the final way that writing process can help us get unstuck. Understanding how we work as writers expands our definition of success to include intrinsic satisfaction as well as external validation. The typical definition of scholarly success, the one that is demanded by most scholars' institutions, is focused on productivity and external reward: Publication. Fellowships and grants. Publicity. Awards. These outcomes are meaningful, for they acknowledge our skill and expertise. But the fact is that external rewards are limited in their significance and positive impact. The most powerful rewards—the ones that have the strongest and most long-lasting effect on motivation and persistence—are internal ones like the satisfaction that comes from a job well done (Amabile & Kramer, 2011). Once we are clearer on our process, we can plan for and achieve the incremental progress that helps produce that sense of satisfaction. But even with the writing process model under our belt, it's a challenge to make use of it without first transforming the abstract model into specific strategies we can use in our writing sessions. The next chapter explains one powerful way to do exactly that.

Focus Point

1. Which of these stages of the writing process is easiest for you?
2. Which always causes you trouble?
3. Which stages create problems you're always able to overcome?

Notes

1. Though see Sword (2017) for counterevidence.

2. Though it's not just academics that feel this: Maya Angelou is reported to have said that "I have written eleven books, but each time I think, 'Uh oh, they're going to find out now. I've run a game on everybody and they're going to find me out.'

3. In addition, Flower (1980) shows that even in an assigned piece of writing, it's the writer's decision-making and redefinition of the problem contained in the assignment that distinguishes the quality of the work; not whether the topic is externally assigned.

4. Saturation might not be consciously dedicated to the production of a particular manuscript. For example, I engaged in a long period of Saturation when I became interested in writing process. It wasn't until someone else suggested to me that I consider writing a book that Saturation became purposeful and began to have a shape around it.

5. All But Dissertation, the point at which a PhD student has completed all coursework and exams and has only to complete and defend the dissertation before being awarded a PhD.

6. Scholars tend to erroneously think of this moment as some sort of test of the "rightness" of everything that has gone before. And it's true, the overt entrance of another reader into our orbit can make this stage *feel* more meaningful for the writer. But the fact is, none of these characteristics makes Clarification a more meaningful part of the writing process. This part of the process is entirely impossible if we don't give the right amount of attention to the previous parts.

7. I've observed that for some scholars, Submission is almost a part of Clarification—that is, they have to talk to other people to get clarity about what they're trying to say.

8. And while vacations can involve a pause from work routines, they are not necessarily restorative. Especially when they include one's entire family, they can include other forms of domestic labor that may be as taxing. Multiple studies have also shown that the positive effects of vacation on health and well-being tend to disappear within a week of returning to work (Nawijn et al., 2010; de bloom et al., 2013).

9. As I did, when we first started working together. This was one of many lessons I received from clients on how writing process and best practices don't always get along.

Finding the Writer Inside

How to Get Unstuck and Start Writing Again

"'What if I'm not a good enough writer?' Ah. She doubts. She doesn't believe it. She craves being taken seriously but she won't do that for herself."

–Sidney Stark, *The Guernsey Literary and Potato Peel Pie Society*

It seems sort of magical, no? This quiet, hidden bank of knowledge that's all your own—already a part of who you are and how you do things. Just waiting for you to notice it, so you can rocket your way to the top of your field. The notion of the writing process has this fairy-tale quality to it, and it's easy to imagine ourselves as the princess raised by farmers, who will one day discover her birthright and return to her rightful place on the throne. What is it then, that keeps us from drawing on this knowledge when we need it most? If the writing process is so central to us, so inherently ours, and so core to what we do, shouldn't we be able to see it naturally and use it immediately? The way I talk about it, it seems like the writing process would make a book about being stuck unnecessary.

This was the dilemma Jameelah was struggling with in her second year on the tenure track. The nice thing about her department was how close everybody was. Everyone worked at least part of the day in their campus office—and they kept their office doors open too. It was a little weird in fact if you closed it for anything other than a meeting. That meant when she got stuck, she could always just pop her head into a colleague's office and run a few ideas past them.

She felt comfortable talking about half-formed ideas, even with more senior colleagues. They'd have these great, wide-ranging conversations and she'd get tons of advice about how to move forward. In just half an hour she'd be pumped up with excitement about her project and have a half dozen different ideas she could pursue to help her move her work forward.

It was great. And also . . . a problem. Once she'd return to her office, she'd jump back into the manuscript and start down a new line of thought. But then a week or two later, she'd realize she'd gone off the rails. What was her original question again? And how was it related to any of this new stuff she'd done? Did any of these new ideas actually help her solve the problem she began with? She'd feel even more confused at that point. And not just confused. Anxious, as well, because she'd "wasted" so much time.

The reason it was so hard for Jameelah to draw on her writing process is because knowledge of it often comes in a form that is difficult to access. As scholars, we're used to having large stores of knowledge at our fingertips. The foundational formulas, precepts, contexts, and principles of our fields are on the tips of our tongues, and what we forget is easily refreshed with a glance at a favorite source. Yet, the writing process isn't an idea waiting at the ready; it's a way of doing things, one that's often hidden in our bodies. Not a glittering jewel flashing on our fingers. More like a treasure buried in our bones. Finding and using this treasure requires us to, as Sidney Stark suggests in the opening epigraph, take ourselves seriously. Even if no one else does. But it's much easier to do so if we understand why our hidden treasures are so difficult to find.

So, in this chapter, we'll begin by understanding why it's so difficult to draw on writing process even though it's ours. Then I'll share how you can use a Writing Metaphor to uncover your process. This strategy requires us to dig a little, in a way that might feel unfamiliar. But it leads to a rich, rewarding clarity about who you are as a writer. Your Writing Metaphor will raise your awareness of what you do at different stages of the writing process and which of those activities are working well for you. It will also show you, just as clearly, what is *not* working for you. If finding out this information causes you some distress, try not to worry: the last section of this chapter (along with Chapter 5) provides suggestions for how to manage that situation. These portions of the book will help you discover that what seems like a quirk or a weakness is often an unrecognized strength.

Why It's Hard to Draw on Process

Several things make it difficult to follow our natural writing process. The first is that a writing process is often a form of tacit knowledge. Tacit knowledge is that thing that we know without recognizing we know it, or even being able to articulate what we know when asked about it (Eraut, 2000; Wagner & Sternberg, 1985; Schön, 2016). We often pick up tacit knowledge "accidentally"—take, for example, the way we learned slang when we were in high school, and how we knew when certain words were out of style. There was no unit in English class devoted to teaching this material. Instead, we learned from consuming popular culture and from observing the behavior of popular students about what was hip and what was not.

Education scholars call this way of gaining knowledge "implicit learning," the kind that takes place when there is "no awareness of learning at the time it takes place" (Eraut, 2000, p. 12). Implicit learning often happens through observation of certain contexts. For example, when you move from one school to the next and start using the word "sick" instead of "cool" to describe something good. It can also take place when we're engaged in certain activities (e.g., you're shopping with friends at the mall and come to understand that flattop docksiders are "for girls," while roundtop docksiders are "for boys"). One way to think about it then, is that tacit knowledge includes the "invisible and automatic insights, experiences, and decision-making criteria people develop in response to learning how to navigate the world around them" (Peet, n.d., p. 5).

We often develop our writing process that way—over time, through experience, and without being conscious that we're learning anything at all. Unlike the concepts, theories, and methods we discuss extensively in graduate seminars, the writing process is something we often figure out through experimentation. We try things out in conference papers—tossing what fails us and sticking with what works. You might also pick up parts of your writing process through observing and participating in the culture of your department. Jameelah is a perfect example of that—she learned to shop her ideas around early on. Doing so is a great habit, one that's often difficult to convince junior scholars to engage in. But she needed to time this habit differently in order for it to work to her advantage (see Chapter 5).

It's also possible that we might pick up parts of our writing process from an advisor or mentor—not because they directly articulate what to do, but because they model certain strategies for handling the challenges of writing. Think, for example, about the graduate student who is lucky enough to co-author a piece with an advisor, who spends a year exchanging drafts and working through puzzles together. This is also an instance of implicit learning: without directly instructing their graduate student on how to do so, the advisor may model for them how to efficiently read the literature or bounce back and respond to harsh reviews and rejections. By doing so, the professor not only offers a set of strategies to incorporate into the student's writing process—but also normalizes the process of hitting roadblocks and builds the student's confidence in their ability to move past them.

And yet, we can also develop the tacit knowledge of our writing process through more formal learning situations, such as those that take place in a classroom. Anyone who learned in high school to outline their arguments before writing has experienced this kind of learning. In this instance, we receive explicit instructions on how to do something. Yet the things we learn become so ingrained that we are no longer able to explain why or how we do them. These experiences occur over time and combine to form a tacit knowledge base we can draw from for years (Eraut, p. 13). Yet we often aren't even aware that we're doing anything particular at all—and certainly not something that we can think of as a set of skills or strategies to be drawn on in times of trouble. It's that lack of awareness that makes it so hard to make our writing process an ally.

A second reason it's so hard to draw upon our writing process is that we're often ashamed to ask for the help we need to uncover it. By the time we've entered graduate school, many of us feel we should already know everything there is to know about turning an idea in our heads into coherent, well-organized, well-argued words on the page. It's as if we assume that what we learned in high school and college should be enough to prepare us for the *process* of writing as a scholar. Of course, this doesn't line up with how we think about the rest of our professional skills—we don't assume that our under-graduate education prepared us for doctoral-level teaching, research, collegial-ity, diplomacy, or administrative skills. Nor do we expect to have mastered all the style or structure of scholarly writing. Yet many of us feel that once we understand the grammar (the rules that guide the correct use of a language) we should also understand our process (the "rules" that guide our most effective method of unearthing and expressing ideas).

I often encounter this assumption in scholars who have a relatively happy relationship with their writing and have trouble understanding what I mean when I say I'm a writing coach.[1] More significant, however, is that scholars who struggle with their writing *also* assume that they should already know how to follow their writing process. Unlike their more easeful colleagues, they are not as likely to articulate this struggle, because they feel ashamed of having missed what they're sure was an essential lesson of their graduate training. Yes, scholars will tell me, they've published articles in the highest-ranking journal in their field. They may be tenured, full, or endowed. "But I never really learned how to write," they will say. "I don't know what I'm doing," they confess. "What's wrong with me that I need a writing coach?" they ask, their faces flushed. While the scholars who are in a happy relation-ship with their writing feel relatively free to assert that the writing process is something we all learned long ago, the troubled writers are silently tormented and deeply shamed by this same assumption, which makes it difficult to find the resources they need to support themselves.

A third pattern I see that prevents scholars from drawing on their writing process is a lack of self-trust. Even when they have a hunch about what they need to do, scholars will often doubt themselves, even adopting an oppo-site approach from the one that works for them, especially if it's been rec-ommended to them by someone trusted, admired, or more experienced than themselves. Elison is a perfect example of this pattern—he was "an outliner," as he called himself, someone who needed to order his thoughts in hierarchi-cal bullet form before he could make progress. But because that technique was something he had learned in high school, and because it often took a long time, he abandoned it, assuming there was something "juvenile" about it and that he was "wasting his time." As we saw in Chapter 2, this loss of trust can happen when we get stuck in our writing. But we don't need to be stuck for this lack of confidence to rear its head. Even scholars who are writing regularly and with relative ease may doubt or forget strategies that once worked for them in the past—in part because it's so hard to even be aware of our process.

If tacit knowledge were just a "bonus" skill—something extra that just made the process a little smoother, perhaps the difficulty in accessing it wouldn't be so significant. It might be tempting to dismiss the notion of tacit knowledge as an "extra" insight that serves mostly to make the journey from graduate student to full professor a little easier. But awareness of our writing process is central to our professional success and has real meaning for the rewards we receive as scholars. Wagner and Sternberg show, for example, that the level of tacit knowledge of both faculty and graduate students impacted scholars' professional performance. Those with more tacit knowledge enjoyed more publications, were more frequently cited, attended more conferences, and were more likely to be employed in high-prestige departments (Wagner & Sternberg, 1985, p. 452). My experience as a coach suggests that awareness of the writing process has the same significance for professional success and personal satisfaction.

This link between tacit knowledge and professional success is even more significant when we consider the unequal access junior scholars have to support that makes uncovering and refining a writing process easier. Like everything else in the academic apprenticeship system, the extent to which you learn from others about the process depends on your relationships with advisors and mentors. As a result, not everyone is going to receive the same training and support in uncovering their writing process. Even if you're a professor who loves writing and longs to help your students, the tacit nature of your knowledge can make it very difficult to clearly convey the lessons you've learned. Tacit knowledge is "disorganized, informal, and relatively inaccessible, making it potentially ill-suited for direct instruction" (Wagner & Sternberg, 1985, p. 439). This is part of the reason that advisors' explicit suggestions about writing can devolve into an extremely well-intentioned, but sometimes unhelpful version of "Do this—it works for me!"[2]

If we're lucky as graduate students, we come across professors who share their tacit knowledge, but offer it as an option, not a directive. If we're *very* lucky, they also model certain parts of the writing process for us—still a form of implicit learning, but at least one that doesn't leave us to figure everything out on our own. The charmed among us find an advisor who thinks deeply about the writing process, communicates directly to us about it, and encourages us to honor our process rather than blindly adopting theirs. But this sort of direct, continuous instruction about the writing process is extremely rare.[3] Luckily, the strategy for uncovering the writing process is simple, one with which all scholars are familiar from our roles as both students and teachers.

How to Uncover Your Writing Process

One of the most effective ways of uncovering our writing process is through the simple act of reflection. Reflection is nothing more than the careful consideration of experience, an "in-depth review of events . . . to bring experience into focus from as many angles as possible" (Bolton, 2014, p. 7). Engaging in this kind of review can take our ephemeral, hidden knowledge of our writing process and make it explicit, clear, and usable. How? First, reflection directs our attention to the factors that generate our experience (Matthew & Sternberg, 2009). That is, reflection makes us pay attention to what we're doing when we write, even small things we wouldn't necessarily notice. The cup of tea, the doodling, the walk around the block. All these subtle aspects of our process become clearer once we give them our attention.

A second reason reflection helps uncover our process is it helps us focus on the assumptions behind what we do (Matthew & Sternberg, 2009). Your epigraph; your outline; your colored pens; your marginalia. Why do they seem like the next best step for you? And when don't they seem to make sense? Having a clearer understanding of the elements and assumptions behind what we do creates what Sternberg refers to as a "condition-action map." In other words, it gives us information about what are "appropriate responses under particular environmental conditions." We can think of our writing process as a hidden "rule book" we use without realizing it. Reflection helps us lay out those rules explicitly so that we're better able to draw on our tacit knowledge to solve our writing problems. There are multiple models of reflection with varying degrees of effectiveness (Matthew & Sternberg, 2009; Bolton, 2014, pp. 44–65). Yet, there's one I've found to be exceptionally effective in uncovering the writing process: the development of the Writing Metaphor.

Simply defined, a metaphor is a figure of speech in which one thing is described in terms of another, to suggest a likeness between them. Metaphors are extremely useful for helping us uncover tacit knowledge because they help us see the world anew, in three different ways. First, metaphors help us describe key aspects of a thing by comparing it to something else. "Writing is an act of faith, not a trick of grammar," says *Stuart Little* author E. B. White. With this metaphor, he suggests that the real work of writing lies not in technical skill, but in our ability to stay committed to a mysterious and challenging process in the absence of confirmation that we're doing the right thing. Compare White's metaphor to John Gregory Dunne's, who asserts that "writing is manual labor of the mind: a job, like laying pipe." This vision of writing strips it of its romance and emphasizes the aspects of writing that, like any other job, involve skill, repetition, and the unerring commitment to showing up day after day. In his autobiography *American Hunger*, Richard Wright reminds us that, regardless of what it feels like for the author, writing is essentially a relational act, an attempt to be seen and heard: "I wanted," says Wright, "to try to build a bridge of words between me and that world outside, that world that was so distant and elusive that it seemed unreal." Each of these authors' metaphors is different. Neither is "right" nor "wrong." Instead, each illuminates some essential element of writing, so that we better understand its nature. Writing Metaphors can also help us better understand *our* nature as writers. Not only can they change our beliefs about writing, but they can also help us build stronger writing identities (Perrow, Feldstein, & Sieler, 2020; Sword, 2017, 2019).

Not only can metaphor help us *describe* what we already know about our experience; but it can also *reveal* or clarify the dimensions of the phenomenon we're trying to understand. As Donald Schön and others point out, a new scientific theory is often modeled on existing theories—that is, researchers try to understand how something works (and how it can work better) by drawing on what they already know about different but related phenomena: take, for example, the case of "physicists modeling theories of sound waves on existing theories of waves in liquids" (Schön, 2016, p. 183). Schön refers to this as "seeing-as," the act of thinking of one thing as an instance of another, in such a way that we learn something new about the first. "What makes the process one of metaphor making rather than simply describing," asserts Schön, "is that the new putative description already belongs to what is initially perceived as a different, albeit familiar thing; hence everything one knows about [the first thing] has the potential of being brought into play in this redescription of [the second thing]" (2016, p. 185). In other words, the comparison object in a metaphor is useful precisely because we already understand it.

Finally, metaphors help us "express the inexpressible" (Nonaka, 1991, p. 99). That is, metaphor helps us *communicate* ideas and experiences we might otherwise be unable to convey. Scientists, for example, use metaphor to help lay people grasp difficult concepts or phenomena. "The physicist Feynman described a drop of water magnified 2,000 times as a teeming football match, and the operation of electromagnetic fields as two corks floating in water (1995)" (Bolton, 2014, p. 105). In the case of scientists, the difficulty lies in the limits of human ability to conceptualize or imagine the phenomenon in question. Metaphors can do the same thing for writers, by helping us capture, not just what writing is, but how writing *feels*. Margaret Atwood's exploration of this topic provides a haunting illustration of what writing is like. When she asked novelists what it felt like when they went "into" a novel,

> None of them wanted to know what I meant by into. One said it was like walking into a labyrinth, without knowing what monster might be inside; another said it was like groping through a tunnel; another said it was like being in a cave—she could see daylight through the opening, but she was in darkness. Another said it was like being underwater, in a lake or ocean. Another said it was like being in a completely dark room, feeling her way: she had to rearrange the furniture in the dark, and then when it was all arranged the light would come on. . . . Obstruction, obscurity, emptiness, disorientation, twilight, blackout, often combined with a struggle or path or journey—an inability to see one's way forward, but a feeling that there was a way forward, and that the act of going

forward would eventually bring about the conditions for vision—these were the common elements in many descriptions of the process of writing. (Atwood, 2002, pp. xxii–xxiii)

This element of writing—our emotional and psychological *sense* of the experience—is especially important for writers to apprehend. Every writer must be able to recognize and face these sensory challenges if we ever hope to overcome them. But scholars need to pay special attention to them. That's because we operate within a professional culture that either ignores the emotional elements of writing or questions the competence and grit of those who confess to them. This kind of shaming makes it even more difficult to develop the skills and resources necessary to help scholarly writers move past these barriers.

My own experience in developing the writing metaphor as an exercise illustrates two powers of metaphor—its ability to describe and reveal key aspects of an experience (Boyd, 2012). In 2003, when I was in my second year as a faculty member, I was part of a writing accountability group and consistently failed to meet my writing goals during the first few semesters I participated in the group. Each week, I would accomplish a significant amount of work, yet by the end of the semester, I always fell short of what I had set out to do. After extensive discussion with group members, I realized that I had no sense of what was a reasonable goal given my own writing pace. Patterning myself on my colleagues or writing group members was pointless—both my department and my writing group were multidisciplinary, and their members varied too widely in discipline, seniority, productivity, and genre to serve as a reasonable model for my output. Moreover, I sensed even then that, had I been able to find a suitable model, using some other scholar's process and pace as a benchmark for my own would only lead to unhealthy comparison and useless competition. After yet another meeting focused on this problem, my fellow group members suggested that one of my goals for the following week be to determine how long it takes for me to draft a journal-length article while teaching the standard 2:2 course load at my university.

It's important to remember that my original purpose was not to *develop an analogy* for the writing process. Rather, my assignment was to *devise a time estimate*. Yet I soon realized that one reason I could not accurately estimate the time required to draft an article is that I could not define a draft. That is, I was using the word "draft" inconsistently. Sometimes the word referred to a confused and convoluted collection of big ideas that I showed to very close colleagues in the hope that a second eye would help clarify my thinking. At other times a draft was a more polished piece of work ready to be seen by more distant colleagues—those whose experience and expertise made them excellent sources of feedback, but to whom I was unwilling to expose my flaws. I also used the word draft to refer to the finished piece of work I submitted to refereed journals, but which I expected to revise after receiving feedback from reviewers. Which was I referring to at any given time? More importantly, what kind of work was required to produce each one? I knew I had to write, of course, but had no idea what took place when I wrote. All three kinds of drafts differed in purpose, scope, and polish. What was involved in working on each kind of draft? What did progress look like for me? Did I work in stages, or circle through the same process over and over? How and when did I capture ideas? Develop arguments? Narrow down claims? Or reconcile inconsistencies? Like many scholars, I'd never purposefully considered these questions.[4]

In my attempt to understand what a draft was, I began laying out the stages of creation and began to see the process as akin to the gestation and birth of a human baby. It was at this point that I began the process of "seeing-as" that Schön describes. Laying out its stages helped me see one of the key elements of writing: that manuscripts were a thing that grew, over time, and were *naturally and necessarily undeveloped* early on in the process. While this point might seem obvious, it is one that I ignored and my retreat participants regularly dismiss, even though we know it makes no sense to do so: we should not expect the level of polish and substance in the beginning stages of the manuscript that we do at the end. Nor should we assume that our work will never be any good in its beginning stages. Yet we do so, again and again.

Laying out the stages of a draft also helped me reveal hidden dimensions of my writing process: who knew that the final, administrative tasks of manuscript submission—the editing, titling, and press communications—could take such a long time and require such focus? What this initial draft of the writing metaphor did not help me do was capture the ineffable—those inexpressible and unfaceable fears that we can't even express to ourselves, much less anybody else. Focused as I was on productivity as the best and most important indicator of writing success, my primary focus was on the amount of time each phase of writing would take so that I could better meet my deadlines.

Since first designing this metaphor exercise, I have taught it to more than a thousand scholars—in large and small workshops, as well as in one-on-one coaching sessions. It's this work that taught me that no understanding of the writing process is complete without attending to the fears and anxieties that underlie our writing. What I heard over and over again from these scholars (and what I later found repeated in the literature) was that writing could terrify and immobilize them. That these feelings caused them great shame. And worst of all—that they felt that they were the only ones feeling this way. It was in response to this realization that I expanded my original Metaphor exercise to more directly elicit the emotional dimensions of writing.

The remainder of this chapter describes the latest version of the Writing Metaphor exercise and draws on the metaphors developed by former workshop participants, retreaters, and coaching clients to illustrate what the process looks like. Creating a metaphor involves five steps:

Step 1: Describe your experience of writing

Step 2: Identify the stages of your writing experience

Step 3: Characterize the writing at each stage of the metaphor

Step 4: Describe your response to each stage of the metaphor

Step 5: Follow your process every time you write

It's important to remember that there is no way to create a Writing Metaphor that's "bad" or "wrong." The goal of this exercise is not to capture some absolute truth that will lay out an unerring map toward professional success. Instead, the goal of this exercise is to raise your awareness of how you work as a writer—so you can better understand what brings you pleasure, what gives you satisfaction, what gets in your way, and how you can move past it. It's not unusual for scholars to complete this exercise and realize they're better equipped to overcome barriers than they thought they were. That same scholar might be overcome by sadness when they realize how trapped they've felt by an activity they used to love. They might also feel dismayed to find there are one or two ways they repeatedly get stuck and have no idea how to overcome that challenge.

In other words, this exercise is likely to generate emotional responses, not just intellectual insights. Writing Metaphors can be incredibly revealing, uncovering aspects of your process that you never paid attention to, and offering solutions to troubles that have bedeviled you for years. They can also stir up your worries by making plain the problems that get in your way, without offering immediately obvious solutions. Later sections provide hints on what to do if feelings arise that threaten to derail you. It's also helpful to remember that the Writing Metaphor is a lens, not a conviction. Any revelation it brings you about your writing process is a win—even if it's uncomfortable. And will ultimately bring you closer to being able to manage your stuck moments with greater ease and courage.

Step 1: Describe Your Experience of Writing

To uncover the hidden aspects of your writing process, we need to go beyond our conventional assessments and judgments of it, and instead create a picture of the whole experience. This includes not just the intellectual elements of writing but its emotional aspects as well. The first step then, in creating a metaphor, is to describe it to yourself in both emotional and intellectual terms. We do this by answering the question, "What does writing feel like to you?" In considering this question, you're doing two things: First, you're starting with the emotional and sensory dimensions of writing rather than its cognitive or social dimension. In doing so, you're countering the (understandable) tendency among many scholars to think analytically and bypass the issue of felt experience. Second, you're taking your first step on the path to "seeing-as." That is, you're using what you know about one thing (the thing that your writing is "like") to help you understand what's happening with the other (your writing).

It helps when describing what writing feels like to begin with an initial image or experience and describe it in great detail. For example, Raphaëlle Rabanes, an assistant professor of Anthropology at the University of Washington, describes writing as the process of "installing lights or paintings in a room. Maybe curating a collective art exhibit."[5] Even this simple statement suggests a lot about what writing might feel like to her: there's a selection process, and it involves other people, as well as some sort of presentation, and the attempt to make the work visible to others. Yet, see how much additional information we get when Raphaëlle continues with the description of the curation process. She goes on to describe what curating this type of exhibit involves:

> Drawing some images, reworking them because I want to integrate new elements (even collage), framing them, hanging them, also choosing other people's art that I want to be in conversation with, finding the right light to showcase each of them, and finding the right order to arrange them so that they resonate with each other. Then, writing actual show notes: bringing the art pieces together with an introductory statement, but it appears afterward, once I have felt how things fit together. At some point, things intuitively fit together, and I feel ready to invite other people to the show.

With this more robust description, we have a sense not only of what the selection and presentation process look like. We also have a hint of what order Raphaëlle's work appears in: the introduction doesn't happen until after she understands the connections between the parts. And even this understanding isn't intellectual for her. It is "felt" intuitively rather than assessed analytically. In other words, the key work at this stage of the exercise is to describe in as much detail as possible whatever analogy best represents your felt experience of writing.

Focus Point

Be sure to use a metaphor that describes the experience of completing a project. Resist the urge to focus on a disasterizing metaphor that has no good end.

Step 2: Identify the Stages of Your Writing Experience

The next step is to identify the stages of the writing experience by breaking the metaphor down into the discrete parts that make it up. Depending on how detailed your initial description of your metaphor was in Step 1, there may be little else to say. But even the most robust description tends to be more of an overview, one that misses the details that matter. Once you begin to consider what you do when engaging in your metaphor, small, necessary steps become apparent. The first step of Raphaëlle's art exhibit, for example, is "buying material." Of course! It seems obvious now. But it isn't until she breaks the metaphor down into pieces that such small steps become clear.

It's important during this step to be sure that you are describing the *metaphor*, not the writing. That's because, as Schön points out, the power of a metaphor, what makes it a generative tool, is that we are using something we already know a lot about (curating an exhibit) to help us better understand the thing we're finding challenging (writing). So, in this step, we want to "mine the metaphor," examining its elements in great detail, in anticipation of what it will eventually tell us about writing. For Raphaëlle, the steps of curating the collective art exhibit include:

1. Buying the material

2. Bringing it home

3. Unpacking it and setting up

4. Drawing the images

5. Reworking/collage

6. Framing

7. Choosing other people's art

8. Arranging the order in the room

9. Hanging

10. Stepping back and rearranging

11. Installing light/showcasing

12. Preparing show notes

13. Invite other people

14. Welcome people in

Once again, it's crucial to remember that this description is unique to *you*. Perhaps you look at Raphaëlle's list and imagine things you would add (making a list of materials before purchasing; building the frames from scratch). The point is not to include every possible step that every person on the planet would name. The point is to write down whatever steps occur to you, the ones that seem most relevant and obvious. As you'll see later, your Writing Metaphor is a living thing, and you'll have many opportunities to expand or revise it throughout your life as a writer.

● **Focus Point**

Not sure of the steps you take at any given moment? Leave a blank space and come back to it later. Working through the later steps will often give you insight into the earlier steps.

Step 3: Characterize the Writing at Each Stage of the Metaphor

Now is the moment when you begin to uncover what your metaphor has to tell you about your writing. In this step, you want to describe what the writing looks like for you in each stage of the metaphor. We do this by describing three features of the writing.

Writing Tasks: The first feature is the set of tasks you engage in at each stage. Imagine for a moment that you are Raphaëlle, and you are "buying the material." For you, that might be purchasing a fresh notebook in which to make handwritten notes and a few new Muji pens with which to write. It could be writing down all your initial thoughts on the topic on index cards or doing a single-term JSTOR search and a bunch of articles to review. For Raphaëlle, the writing tasks involved in her first few steps include:

1. Buying material—fieldwork/selecting literature

2. Bringing it home—writing field notes/reading articles and highlighting

3. Unpacking it and setting up—coding data/extracting article quotes in bookends

One thing to notice about the first few writing tasks of Raphaëlle's metaphor is that they *include the research*. This is neither required nor preferred when you're creating your metaphor. But in doing so, Raphaëlle's metaphor serves as an important reminder that she is writing while she researches.

Strength of Argument: The second feature to describe in this step is the Clarity of the Argument. A well-constructed argument "is a coherent series of statements in which the author leads the reader from certain premises to a particular conclusion" using claims and evidence (Belcher, 2009, p. 83). In this step, we want to describe the extent to which this happens in each stage of the writing process.

Quality of Writing: The third feature to describe in this step is the Quality of Writing. In other words, whether the text is grammatically correct; whether it's free of spelling errors. Whether the structure of the work (at the level of the sentence, paragraph, section, and chapter) is clear and well organized (Belcher, 2009, p. 171). Whether the style and voice are consistent with and supportive of the message. Because Raphaëlle's metaphor begins with the research, she actually cannot describe these additional features at this stage. But when we move to the later stages of her metaphor, here is what we see:

1. Drawing the images

    a. Writing task: data analysis writing a memo about a theme + formulating thoughts from data

    b. Clarity of Argument: no argument yet, but theme/interest

    c. Clarity of Writing: feels polished because it is intuitive, I love telling stories and following ideas

2. Reworking/collage
   a. Writing task: editing ideas into paragraphs, getting argument out
   b. Intuitive feeling it out, emerging
   c. Loses polish

Dividing the metaphor (and the writing) into different stages and taking the time to describe them in detail illuminates the fact that creating a manuscript requires many different kinds of work. And depending on what stage you're in, that work results in different outcomes with widely varying degrees of polish and completeness. Raphaëlle's example is especially helpful here—even though "reworking/collage" is ostensibly farther along in the process of writing, notice that this stage lacks the polish that exists at earlier stages of the writing. That's because Raphaëlle's love for the work of memoing leads her to create beautifully crafted, richly detailed prose. Yet, she knows that when the time comes to transform description into argument, her writing will "suffer" in the sense that it will be less polished to the outside eye, even as it becomes more of what it needs to be.

This is a simple, even obvious statement about writing: we can't expect the results in the early stages to look like the result we'll see in the later stages. But it's one that the scholars I work with often do not take into account when assessing the quality and outcomes of their work. Instead, I see scholars who hammer away at data analysis, finally cracking open a concept or connection that's tormented them for months—only to report, with downcast eyes, that they "only" have an outline or "haven't done anything" because they can't show their advisor or editor a fully drafted chapter. The writing metaphor helps us take seriously everything that has to happen for us to reach that final, polished stage.

It's helpful to note that, Steps 2 (break the metaphor into stages) and 3 (characterize the writing at each stage) are likely to inform one another. You may begin with a breakdown of your metaphor that feels complete, but once you try to describe the writing task, you'll realize that you missed a step in the metaphor and need to spend time conceptualizing and envisioning it. By the same token, you may find that the steps of your metaphor suggest that you should be engaging in a writing task that heretofore you've not engaged in. Take this back-and-forth relationship between these steps as an opportunity to explore, to play, to imagine. To elaborate your understanding, rather than to live up to an ideal.

Focus Point

This is the "hardest" part of the metaphor—identifying the writing tasks of which you may be least aware. Consider doing this exercise over time and after several writing sessions, observing yourself while you work.

Step 4: Describe Your Response to Each Stage of the Metaphor

Once we have a clear idea of what writing feels and looks like at any given stage, we then explore how we behave when we're in that stage. That's because laying out what writing can look like is not the same as acknowledging what we do when that moment arrives. Step 4 can therefore be stressful because it asks us to return our focus to the behaviors that make us feel stuck. The responses we want to pay attention to are both behavioral and emotional—that is, how we feel is just as important as what we do at any given stage. You might find that your response to the first, beginning stages of your writing process includes a mixture of excitement and anxiety that make you dive into the work obsessively. But that the anxiety becomes stronger when you have to share the work, and instead of diving in, you do anything you can to avoid it. You want to make sure in Step 4 that you describe what you feel and what you do in equal detail. That's because, by naming these responses before you encounter them, you equip yourself to notice them for what they are and respond in ways that you find more useful.

As you dive into these descriptions of how you respond to each phase of writing, it's useful to remember two things: the first is that the information we glean from this step is nothing more than data—it's information that we're gathering to help us better understand what writing looks like for us. And just like any other form of research, all data is welcome—even if it's not what we want to see. The second thing to remember about this step in developing a metaphor, is that it will not only reveal to you when your responses impede your productivity. It will also illustrate what you do that supports your productivity. It's easy to forget this, as we look at ourselves squarely in the mirror and encounter behavior we'd rather not see. But *every writer* has work that comes easily—barriers that barely phase them and strategies so successful that they barely notice them. It's just that we give less attention to these aspects of writing because they go so smoothly.

The metaphor illustrated next is from Renita, a graduate student who attended the metaphor workshop in 2017. In a brief email to me, she described her metaphor and what she'd gleaned about her writing as a result of creating it.[6] I have labeled the sections of her description with the steps each one corresponds to.

[STEP 1: METAPHOR] Writing for me is like preparing for a business trip or conference that I don't want to go to.

[STEP 2: STAGES] I will book the flight, hotel, and print out the trip itinerary and stash it under a pile of junk until I'm ready for it. Weeks go by, maybe even a month or two, until I wake up suddenly at 2:37 am. I'm sweating, my heart is pounding, and I'm frantically trying to pack for the trip. I rush to the pile where all my important travel information is hidden, knock that over to grab what I need, and then rush to the airport.

I get to my final destination, barely. In my haste, I packed toothpaste but no toothbrush, shoes but no socks, and somehow managed to not pack anything to sleep in. The first day is rough, but I make it through. As the trip progresses, I find that I'm enjoying myself. A LOT. I don't want to leave! But.. it's time to head to the airport and head back home.

[STEP 3: CHARACTERIZE (TASKS)]: The preparation stage is where I glance at the assignment requirements and put them away to come back to at some point. That point comes when I realize that my far-away deadline is within the next week or so. The frantic packing stage is where I'm doing most of my writing. It's a frenzied mess of words and thoughts being typed on the screen in Word. When I start to enjoy the trip is when I'm editing my paper and my thoughts are coming together. Because I didn't pack appropriately (find certain sources/create an informed outline), I don't feel as prepared as I could be. The point when it's time to go home is when the assignment is due.

One thing that Renita's description illustrates is that you may find that the responses to each writing phase are *already contained* in Steps 1 and 2. Renita, for example, details how the return to her writing includes a fairly familiar biological panic response. She is "hasty" in her work which is why she is disorganized in her packing. If we were to separate out her responses from the paragraphs, they might look something like this:

1. Book the flight and hotel—glance at the assignment and put it away

2. Weeks go by—**disengage** from the project

3. Wake up suddenly—realize that deadline is near; **sweating, heart pounding**

4. Pack—type a **frenzied** mess of words and thoughts in Word.

5. **Rush** to find travel information and go to the airport; pack incompletely—finding sources, creating an informed outline, but doing so incompletely

6. Trip/conference begins—**rough** but I make it through

7. Trip/conference progresses—I **enjoy myself. A LOT. I don't want to leave!** but **feel unprepared**—edit the paper and thoughts come together

8. Head to the airport and go home—turn in the assignment

Laying out responses in this manner helps to identify exactly what Renita is doing that gets in her way. It also helps alert her to what she can expect when she receives an assignment. Most importantly, it helps distinguish between the practical steps she takes to develop her ideas from the responses she sometimes has when called upon to take those steps.

Focus Point

If you find yourself being harshly critical when describing your responses at each stage of the metaphor, imagine that you are writing up the metaphor of your best friend (you are, actually), and adopt the language and tone that you would use with them.

Filling in the Blanks

If at this point, the state of your metaphor makes you worried, you're not alone. There are two problems that scholars often face at this point in the exploration of their writing that, if not handled properly, can leave them feeling frail rather than empowered. Let's take each one in turn:

The first problem scholars may face is the Enfeebling Metaphor. A scholar at Boston University first raised my awareness of this issue after a workshop in 2019. "What if your metaphor itself *is* the problem?" he asked, going on to explain that the metaphor he'd chosen could do nothing other than end in disaster.[7] This type of metaphor is what Helen Sword describes as a "Splinter" metaphor, one that is "subtly destructive, like tiny splinters that lodge under our skin and fester" (2019, p. 47). The "Splinter" metaphor doesn't just reveal challenging elements of your writing process, as was the case with Renita. The Splinter Metaphor is by its very nature unhelpful—holding little more than negative associations and outcomes, and thereby offering very little insight into the actual dynamics of writing.

When this happens, there are three possible avenues of repair. One strategy is the Positive Probe: in other words, examine the existing metaphor for its helpful and useful dimensions. Here I'm asking you to put as much attention on what's working as you do on what's *not* working. Look back over your metaphor and notice where you feel neutral or even positive feelings about each stage. Are there places where you glossed over the small joys that stage can bring? Are there hard-fought triumphs you eventually experience, even though there are less joyful dimensions to the work? Go back and mine your memory and your metaphor for the jewels hidden under the rubble. The point of this step is not to put a false shine on the experience. The point is to make sure that you have a metaphor that's as evenhanded and accurate as possible, rather than one so soaked in your fears that you can't see straight.

Another strategy I find especially useful is to rework your metaphor around an especially satisfying, especially successful experience of writing. Many times, the Enfeebling Metaphor is based on experiences that are recent and painful. Rather than generating a metaphor based on more typical or positive experiences, an especially stuck scholar might find it difficult to think of anything other than the experience that's most present in their mind, even though it may not be representative. Under these circumstances, I encourage scholars to think back on a time in their lives when writing felt especially good or they performed in a way they were especially proud of. If this means recalling experiences from high school or grammar school, so be it. It might even require asking a friend, colleague, or loved one what they remember about you and your writing at this time. The point here is that if you're caught in an especially tender moment of your writing life, it's helpful to seek out a fuller, more accurate sense of what the writing experience has been and can be like. Generate a writing metaphor centered on this experience and see what new information it reveals.

A final strategy we might use for the Enfeebling Metaphor is to look at the responses that cause us problems and imagine how we might respond differently. For example, after completing her metaphor, Renita informed me of several changes she'd made to her process to help address the patterns that she'd noticed at the workshop.

> As we discussed at the conference, my expectations are higher than my professor and I typically get positive comments and full credit for my work. The first step that I took was to allow myself time to recover after the "packing" stage. This is where I'm connecting thoughts and need some time to subconsciously think about a paper. Breaking that up into smaller chunks has also helped with the stress of the process. My goal is to give myself more time to work on a draft so that it's not a stressed frenzy that leaves me burned out (and unable to start the next project because I'm so tired).

These are changes she made on her own, without any input from me, merely as a result of fleshing out her responses in such a detailed and eye-opening way. Renita's response to her metaphor is a variation on what Helen Sword calls "turning splinters into cobblestones." Sword argues that there are times when "splinters are best prised out with a needle or coaxed to the surface with a hot compress and then discarded. In other cases, however, a negative metaphor can teach us fundamental and ultimately affirmative truths about our writing process" (2019, p. 4). This second strategy is the one that Renita used, digging into the first moment when she got off track and devising one small change that she could make, one that could change the entire course of her metaphor.

Step 5: Follow Your Process Every Time You Write

The final step of developing the Writing Metaphor is to deliberately use the strategies you have uncovered in Steps 1 through 4. While this step might seem obvious, it's helpful to remember that the metaphor often reveals a mountain of new information about how you do what you do. It may continue to do so long after your first attempt to sketch it out, as new strategies reveal new dimensions of the metaphor—or even change it entirely to better capture your experience. That means it won't always occur to you to try out the strategies that you've identified; nor will it necessarily feel natural to try them when it does occur to you. Instead, deliberately drawing on that knowledge to solve your writing dilemmas will require you to actively practice them.

Despite all your efforts, you may find that there are stages of the writing process you just can't figure out how to move through. The strategies you use always seem to take you off track, take longer than you'd like, and create more confusion than you think necessary. You might be wondering what to do instead. If this sounds familiar, the next chapter is for you.

Notes

1. My guess is that these scholars have naturalized their tacit knowledge—seeing it as a function of their personality rather than a learned skill whose acquisition they've forgotten. I've found support for this hypothesis in Boice's work (1993) on blocked writing, where he points out that both fluent and "dysfluent" writers often feel an aversion to writing, especially before beginning. The difference is that fluent writers have learned strategies for managing that aversion and feel confident in their ability to overcome it.

2. But didn't I just say that modeling helps? Certainly. But when scared, stuck scholars are looking for direction, the suggestions from more experienced scholars tend to be taken as law, and students may lack or be afraid to take an experimental approach.

3. I also think there's an argument to be made that professors should not also be saddled with the responsibility of being a writing coach on top of being a subject matter advisor and methods instructor.

4. This unthinking approach to writing is one of the big differences between writers and scholars who write. Most academic writing guides do not explore the meaning of writing for scholars. One exception is Pamela Richards's chapter in Arnold Becker's *Writing for Social Scientists* (1986). Nonacademic writers, by contrast, muse endlessly about the nature of writing and those who do it for a living. Two of the best are Margaret Atwood's *Negotiating With the Dead* (2002), and Annie Dillard's *The Writing Life* (2013).

5. Personal communication, July 17, 2020, via email.

6. Personal communication, May 3, 2017.

7. Personal communication, January 18, 2019.

Growing From the Inside Out

Exploring and Expanding Your Writing Process

"But I had not known that I was strong enough to do any of those things until they were over and I had done them. I had to do the work first, not knowing."

–Naomi Novik, Spinning Silver

The chapter is a mess. I don't know how to start. When I proposed this book last year, chatting gaily about it with my soon-to-be editor, it seemed like it'd be easy, a clever vessel for a collection of ideas I was looking forward to tatting into a coherent whole. Now I curse her silently. I waste several minutes imagining her as Eve in the Garden, then a few more thinking through the misogynist implications of my imagery. I reread what I've written; it's trash. I try diving in at different spots—no go. I read the first few lines of a book I want to sound like, then try to write the chapter so that it sounds like that one. All to no avail. Everything I have to say seems so obvious as to not deserve mention. Actually I don't have any ideas at all, and am not fit to write this book. I'm not going to meet my deadline. In fact, I'm never going to finish. I begin to imagine the look of disappointment on the editor's face. She has a British accent which makes everything she says sound cool when she's happy, but which I imagine will make everything sound more chilling when she's disappointed. Worst of all, I'm writing (that is, *not* writing) a book on writing. I am clearly a fraud and pretty soon everyone is going to know it.

What was especially frustrating about that session was that I don't usually have a hard time getting started. Initiation isn't my big problem—it's more Submission and Hibernation that get in my way. But even when we're longtime friends with our writing process, writing is still . . . writing. And it's not unusual for certain parts of that process to be crystal clear, while others seem like a complete mystery. You know you tend to use highlighters when revising, but have no idea what happens when an idea first comes to you. Perhaps you love drafting—it feels exciting and full of possibility, so you'll draft forever and ever. But once required to move to revisions, you're stumped—clueless as to how to take the mass of writing you've produced and turn it into something usable. What do we do with the parts of our process that are unclear to us? Or that present a problem for which we have no solution? How do we devise new strategies and writing tasks when the ones we're engaged in aren't working?

This is the moment when it's especially tempting to do what others do—to follow *their* process. And while there's nothing wrong with trying out something new, it's easy to get trapped in someone else's strategy, long past the time it's become clear that it doesn't work for us. Even worse is when we start insisting that we "must be doing something wrong" if their strategy isn't effective. It's true, there is no single best practice that works for everyone, all the time. And yet we still need ideas and support from others when we run up against a problem for which we have no ready solution.

When we run into trouble and are searching for a way out, it helps to use a "Practice First" approach: to think of our writing time as a practice session, one in which we deliberately *experiment* with new techniques and strategies to determine how well they work for us. Then, if they show promise, we *practice* them multiple times—repeating, refining, and *customizing* them each time we use them—until they fit just right. This approach to developing a writing process is helpful because it lets us learn from other people without over relying on them. As Novik points out in this chapter's epigraph, we have to try these approaches, even though we're not certain that we're capable of mastering them. It's only through experimentation and customization that we come to know what we can do as writers. By encouraging you to observe and trust your own experience with those strategies, the Practice First approach strengthens your sense of authority over your own writing process.

To help you flesh out your writing metaphor and try the "Practice First" approach to solving writing problems, this chapter provides multiple strategies you can experiment with, summarized in Figure 5.1. For each stage of the writing process, it describes Core Fears that often plague writers; Common Pitfalls we fall into; and one Essential Skill we can develop to help avoid those pitfalls. I purposefully name the Essential Skill before providing specific techniques, so you can think through two questions: first, is this a skill you agree you need to develop? And second, do you already have ways of enacting that skill that you may have forgotten about? I often find that once scholars begin thinking about their writing challenges in terms of concrete skills (instead of personal failings) the strategies that have worked for them will come back in a rush, reducing their need to even experiment with anything else.

Figure 5.1 ● How to Explore and Expand Your Writing Process

Stage	Core Fear	Common Pitfall	Essential Skill	
What stage of your writing process are you in?	Are you feeling this?	Are you doing this?	Have you tried this strategy?	If not, you can experiment with:
Initiation *capturing initial ideas*	I've got nothing worth saying	Devaluing before developing	Purposefully making mistakes	Beautiful Oops
Saturation *immersion in the topic*	I've got to know it all	Endlessly seeking confirmation	Choosing a new audience	Phone-A-Friend
Incubation/Illumination *getting stumped/unstumped*	I'll fall [further] behind	Refusing to stop	Accepting our lack of control	Rest Stops
Clarification *confirming ideas*	I'll get it all wrong	Hiding your work	Taking ideas for a test run	Mock Up the Manuscript
Submission *sharing work*	I'll be found out	Refusing to submit your manuscript	Leading yourself to release	Patch Up & Let Go
Hibernation *regaining energy*	No way that can happen	Pushing past your limits	Immersing yourself in play	Deep Dives Into Delight

Focus Point
THE "PRACTICE FIRST" APPROACH TO SOLVING WRITING PROBLEMS

Rather than assume that someone else's writing process will work for you, deliberately test any suggestion you receive to see how well it works for you.

Step 1: Identify Growth Area
Scan your writing metaphor and find a step for which you don't have a lot of solutions.

Step 2: Find a Strategy
Reflect on whether you have successfully solved this problem in the past. If you haven't, look for suggestions from other sources.

Step 3: Experiment
Try out the strategy during your next writing session and note whether or not it made a difference for you.

Step 4: Practice
Use the strategy the next few times you write to see if its impact is consistent.

Step 5: Customize
Be on the lookout for ways you can tailor the strategy to meet your needs and match your approach.

But if you do need particular techniques to try? You're in luck: there is a vast storehouse of informal and formal knowledge on writing and the creative process that provides many inventive, effective strategies you can use to do the work of writing at any stage in your metaphor. This chapter will draw from that storehouse to suggest strategies you might try. Yet, tried and true as they may be, these new strategies can feel confusing or impossibly risky for a scholar who's feeling especially stuck or especially vulnerable. Ideas that sound delightful and groundbreaking when we come upon them while lounging in the stacks at the library can quickly become overwhelming when we put them into practice. Or perhaps they still sound delightful—but feel too risky given your marginalized status or position in your institution. This is especially the case for strategies that emphasize slowing down, turning in, tolerating imperfection and incompletion, or otherwise rejecting the academic preoccupation with ever-increasing productivity.[1]

Therefore, this chapter builds on and contributes to that storehouse by offering, not just a range of techniques for each moment, but a method for building confidence in each strategy. Drawing from research, from exercises I've designed and successfully used with hundreds of scholars, and from conversations with other writers, this chapter offers a "ladder" of actions you can try out, one that allows you to start small, then build up to more challenging moves. If one of the exercises calls out to you, but feels too intimidating, start with whatever seems easiest. Then, once you feel a bit more confident, you can experiment with the next technique. In addition, this chapter pays particular attention to the moments that scholars and observers of writing process tend to overlook (Incubation, Submission, and Hibernation). These moments, while seemingly the most inconsequential, can seriously impact a scholar's progress and deserve special attention.

Initiation: Purposefully Making Mistakes

You'll remember that the Initiation stage is the moment when an idea first flutters into our head and we attempt to externalize it—to represent those ideas in some form that we can stand apart from. When we think of Initiation, we think of notes scribbled down on cocktail napkins, thumbed into phones, and inked into palms. At first glance, this stage is not one that seems to trouble scholars a lot, at least not directly. This can often be the most enjoyable moment in a writing project: it's interesting, full of possibility, and easy enough to scratch our first thoughts out quickly on the nearest sheet of paper.

Yet, there are times when the act of forming and articulating our "first thoughts" can feel troublesome. If we are wrangling with an emotionally challenging topic, or one that involves a community about whom we feel protective, it can be difficult to allow ourselves to freely state even those initial ideas. What if our ideas hurt someone we care about or challenge someone whose validation and advocacy we need? Initiation also includes the moment when we've moved to a new part of the manuscript—a new chapter or section—and begin the hard work of "starting" all over again. Let's not forget about those moments when we need an idea and don't have one handy—as often happens when we are being asked to join an existing intellectual conversation (Boice, 1994). These moments of Initiation can be compulsory, such as the moment when a graduate student is asked to analyze an idea for a seminar paper. But as you proceed through your career, most of these invitations are optional. You come across a Call for Papers related to your latest project. A group of colleagues asks you to contribute to a panel or round-table. You're asked to speak with a member of the press about the link between your work and current events or discoveries. Each of these can be a starting place, even if the project or body of work they refer to is not new.

Core Fear: Nothing Worth Saying

When Initiation feels difficult, it's often because it feels like a test: a moment when we are called upon to showcase our talents and prove our worth as scholars. Think, for example, about the times when faculty members are asked to provide a written assessment of qualifying exam responses; when they're required to ask questions of grad students during their dissertation defenses; when we are in a seminar or roundtable and feel the pressure—as a participant or as the person leading the discussion—to say something brilliant, or at least as smart as what so-and-so will probably say. These can easily turn into moments during which we feel we need to "come up with something." And not just any old thing. Something that is smart. Interesting. Worthwhile. In other words, the fear that tends to come up around the moment of Initiation is that we don't have any ideas, or certainly not any that are interesting.

Common Pitfall: Devaluing Before Development

The pitfall of this stage is that we will give short shrift to initial ideas before we have had a chance to develop them. Sometimes this happens because the idea seems transgressive. Or it does not seem to "fit" the way our profession or field has thought about a topic in the past. In *Undoing the Silence*, Louise Dunlap describes how scholars' tendency to silence ourselves pops up exactly in the moment when we are on the verge of doing the real work of scholarship: discovering the new and wonderful thing we have to say that distinguishes our work from other's: She notes "Their genuine difficulty in coming out and saying what they knew, especially if it did not mirror what others were saying, their reluctance to affirm their main ideas in simple, direct, accessible words. Rather than being eager to say something new and original, they were, in their way, terrified of sounding different" (Dunlap, 2007, pp. 20–21). Whatever the source of our trepidation, we need to give ourselves adequate time to think through the ideas: to explore them, elaborate them, and see where they might take us if we give them a chance.

Essential Skill: The Beautiful Oops

When in the Initiation stage and facing these fears, one Essential Skill we can develop is to purposefully make mistakes and create a Beautiful Oops.[2] A Beautiful Oops is a messy, mixed-up, mistake-riddled representation of your current thinking that is *intentionally inadequate*. Not only does it capture as much as it can about your current state of thinking. It does so by purposefully pursuing missteps, inappropriate thoughts, impossible leaps of logic, and unclear thoughts. If you're someone who finds it painful enough just to freewrite without editing yourself, you might wonder why I'd encourage such a sloppy, painfully imperfect way of putting your thoughts into words. Why not just start by doing the best that we can? The reason is that making a Beautiful Oops is actually an especially effective and generative strategy for the Initiation stage, for several reasons.

First, the Beautiful Oops gets all your ideas out in front of you. Later on in the writing process, when we're eager to home in on that brilliant one-line description of our argument, multiple ideas can feel like a hindrance. But at this beginning stage of writing, it's useful to entertain lots of options—especially if you're feeling nervous and unable to start. Being willing to play with lots of ideas frees you up as a writer. By deliberately putting all the unfinished, imperfect, inadequate ideas down and treating them as valid, you give yourself more material to play with, especially if you are feeling nervous about your ideas.

The Beautiful Oops doesn't just boost the quantity of ideas available to you. It also improves the quality of your work—by clarifying the weaknesses of both your arguments and the arguments of those with whom you disagree. These weaknesses are something we will eventually have to understand, articulate, and respond to in public. But in order to do that with confidence, we must do so first in private. Making Beautiful Oopses bakes the ability to do so directly into our writing process. And when it's working at its best, it does so early enough to build confidence in our ability to face criticism.

A final reason the Beautiful Oops is so useful? It creates avenues for further exploring our ideas. When Oopsing, you're not trying to come up with the perfect idea. Instead, you're just coming up with a starting point that, *because of what is wrong with it*, provides a useful way to determine what you really want to say. As Daniel C. Dennett points out, deliberately making mistakes is a long-used and effective strategy for figuring out how to get to where you want to go. He explains that, long before GPS, navigators used to determine their position at sea by making a guess about where they were, then calculating where the sun would be in the sky if their initial guess was correct. If it turns out the sun wasn't exactly in that position, it wasn't a fail—instead,

> this told them how big a correction, and in what direction, to make to their initial guess. In such a method it is useful to make a pretty good guess the first time, but it doesn't matter that it is bound to be mistaken; the important thing is to make the mistake, in glorious detail, so there is something serious to correct. (Dennett, 2014, pp. 24–25)

What's true for navigating the ocean is also true for navigating ideas: the better able we are to pick a place to start, the easier it is for us to move in the direction we'd like to go.

Try It Out: How to Oops

Here are a few ways to make a Beautiful Oops when you're in the Initiation stage of writing—and to make one that is clear, precise, and detailed so that you have something to react to. The first tier of suggestions includes strategies that involve writing down whatever you're thinking, without asking you to make "mistakes." The second tier moves on to bona fide Oopses, where you will deliberately write what you think is wrong, in order to give yourself a place to start.

Tier I: Getting It Out

Free-write: Popularized by Peter Elbow, free-writing involves writing whatever comes into your head about your topic for short bursts of time (five minutes is a good starting point), without stopping for anything: not to think through a thought, reread, revise, or correct spelling or grammar. Once you've finished, review your free-writing and circle the most interesting ideas in your text. Free-write for five more minutes about each of those ideas, explaining what makes each one so strong.

FAQ: A variation on free-writing is to create a Frequently Asked Questions document for your ideas. Instead of trying to work in paragraphs or outlines, write down the questions that you are implicitly asking and free-write an answer to each one. Then review your answers to see if they spawn new questions. If so, repeat the exercise from the beginning.

Tier II: Getting It "Wrong"

Opposites Attract: Select one assertion you plan to make, then write down in great detail the exact opposite idea. You can write multiple opposing views, or you can concentrate on one and describe the multiple pieces of evidence supporting it. If it helps, take on the persona of a scholar that you know is in opposition to your ideas and draft what you think they would say. Once you're done, craft your response to their position.

Don't Quote Me on That: Find an epigraph that *contradicts* an important aspect of your manuscript—a basic assumption, a core argument, an experience—anything that seems essential to your thinking. Now, imagine you agree with the contradictory epigraph and explain the ideas behind it. Write down why those ideas are the only reasonable ones to hold. Clearly lay out why anyone who disagrees with the epigraph is a fool. Once you're done, revert to your true opinion: go through the paragraph and lay out all the ways you disagree and the evidence for your position.

Saturation: Choosing a New Audience

Saturation, you'll remember, is the phase in which we're diving into and trying to soak up as much as possible about our research topic. For scholars, this includes the informal, seemingly magical situation in which our topic of interest suddenly appears everywhere we turn. As Donald Murray points out,

> Once a writer decides on a subject or accepts an assignment, information about the subject seems to attach itself to the writer. The writer's perception apparatus finds significance in what the writer observes or overhears or reads or thinks or remembers. The writer becomes a magnet for specific details, insights, anecdotes, statistics, connecting thoughts, references. The subject itself seems to take hold of the writer's experience, turning everything that happens to the writer into material. (1978, p. 376)

Yet, Saturation also includes formal methods of collecting the information with which we will work: writing formulas. Diving into archives. Doing surveys, interviews, and fieldwork. Collecting samples. And of course, for all disciplines and interdisciplines, the quintessential expression of Saturation is the literature review.[3]

The literature review is a continuation of the "conversation" we were invited to during the Initiation stage (Boice, 1994). Think of it this way: Initiation is the moment when you pass by the circle of people talking in the back of the conference room, and hear an idea that grabs your attention, sparks your curiosity, and prompts you to jot down some notes on the back of your conference folder. The literature review, on the other hand, is when you slow down your gait, and one of the people in the circle steps back to make room for you to join in. It sounds lovely when I put it like that doesn't it? But of all the moments in the writing process, writing the literature review is one that seems to most easily raise scholars' anxiety levels.

Core Fear: Knowing It All

One thing that makes this moment especially intimidating is that unlike the scenario I described earlier (which evokes the excitement and fun of an interesting exchange with well-intentioned peers), the way we think and learn about a literature review emphasizes inadequacy—our search to find the failures and false steps in other people's research. When we get caught in this more competitive, defensive experience of Saturation, the giggling game of hide-and-seek can feel like (and turn into) a manhunt: The core questions take on a vicious edge, especially when we have ideological disagreements with the existing body of work. And it can be easy to forget the true purpose of the literature review: which is nothing more than to understand the relationship between the ideas and arguments that make up the conversation to which you want to contribute.

This perpetual hunt for gaps and weaknesses can give the literature review a nasty, competitive, catch-you-out edge. It emphasizes the extent to which our work will be scrutinized by an unsympathetic audience and can foster an overwhelming fear that we will "miss" something. The result is that many scholars are plagued, in the Saturation stage, by two fears. First, that they must know what every scholar before them has ever said on the topic. And second, that once they do know what's been said, they won't have anything to contribute.

Common Pitfall: Endless Pursuit of Confirmation

The fears around knowing it all lead to the classic pitfall of the Saturation stage, which is the endless pursuit of confirmation that you've said it all. What that typically looks like is a tumble down the Reading Rabbit Hole. Is there any scholar who has not felt that desperate certainty that you must read every single publication related to your work, while simultaneously feeling overwhelmed by the prospect of doing so? If you've ever found yourself staring with horror at the findings of a Google Scholar search, then you know what I mean. The problem here is that instead of trying to understand the relationship between the ideas most significant to our question, we slip easily into trying to achieve total mastery of a vast, multidisciplinary, decades-old literature.[4]

Over-reading can prevent us from playing our part in the "conversation." We spend so much time taking in what others say that we don't have a chance to develop our own ideas on the topic. This is at the heart of many a dissertation committee's criticisms: that the student in question knows the work, but has done nothing other than "summarize" the literature, and "doesn't know how to use it for himself." Using our metaphor of the literature review as conversation, the committee member has walked into a party that the student is hosting. She's been invited to sit in one of the chairs set in a circle around the living room. And the student has introduced her committee member to everyone at the party by describing what each person thinks about the topic at hand. The student may even describe how each member of the circle feels about the other. But then the student turns around and abruptly stands up, walks into the kitchen, and waves the advisor over. They then proceed to explain, in a whisper, the study *they* plan to do, without once explaining how their research is connected to that of their other guests.

Essential Skill: Phone-A-Friend

What we need at this stage is to be able to Phone-A-Friend. That is, to purposefully reorient our attention toward a safer audience. Rather than place ourselves in conversation with a person or group we find intimidating, competitive, or actively hostile, we instead, do the opposite: we actively imagine and *write to* a different interlocutor. Someone who is seeking information, is curious, is kind, and is interested. Someone who basically doesn't care if we get it wrong or know only part of the story. Phone-A-Friend allows us to articulate our ideas without restraint, even though they are incomplete and unformed. And once we are willing to let our ideas out, it's easier to clarify the relationship between our ideas and those of others.

Try It Out: How to Phone-A-Friend

Whoever your interlocutor is, be sure that they are an interested audience who listens with curiosity and responds with questions. Try writing out the imaginary "transcript" of a conversation between you and one of the people listed in the next section, where you begin describing your thoughts, then pepper your explanation with the questions you imagine that person might ask. If it works on paper, you might even consider having a live conversation with the person in question.

Tier I: Friends You Love

Letter to Your Mom: I'll be forever grateful to historian Henry Binford, who suggested to me in graduate school that one way to simplify my technical and confused thinking was to write a letter to my mother explaining my argument. To this day, trying to express myself in an informal writing tone, without assuming expert knowledge or relying on jargon remains a staple strategy of mine.

Researcher You to Person You: Ethnographers and other qualitative researchers will recognize this pairing as a version of Memoing, a long-standing, well-regarded technique for capturing initial insights while reading field notes (Emerson, Fretz, & Shaw, 1995). In this strategy, you will read a short piece of your writing that seems especially interesting, but not fully fleshed out—no more than a paragraph or two. Then, adopting the persona of a researcher, write a letter to yourself that describes what's noteworthy about this paragraph. What stands out? What's really fascinating? What patterns do you see? How is what you've written supportive of/similar to/challenging of the work of others? What do you wish you knew more of? This letter is just for you—you never need to show it to anyone else. And its purpose is for you to "hear from" the part of you that's deeply engaged in the work.

Tier II: Friends You Lead

Teacher and Student: In this Friendship, you are expressing your thoughts to someone who lacks expertise and has a decided interest in understanding what you're saying. Taking up the Teacher–Student role pair may be helpful for those who enjoy teaching undergraduates and have a knack for it, as it will slip you more easily into several behaviors such as defining terms, scaffolding concepts, organizing and restating information, and imagining questions and answers.

Coach and Athlete: This pair might be especially helpful for those who are explaining the "how" rather than the why or the what. It's also great if you want to actively role-play with yourself, using whiteboards and diagrams the way you would in a real coaching situation. Is there a physical dimension to what you're explaining? Are you a tactile learner? If you find that moving the body aids your thinking, this Friendship may work for you.

Conductor and Orchestra: This pairing is a different way to express your thinking because instead of explaining what something "is" or what you think, a conductor explains to the orchestra what she wants. What is she looking for? What is missing from the current performance? What needs to be added and how will the orchestra achieve it? Is it an entire section that's off or is it just one person? This pairing is particularly useful for scholars who find a linear arrangement of ideas useless during these initial stages of writing.

Incubation: Accepting Our Lack of Control

Incubation is the period when we stop the conscious attempts to create prose or solve problems and allow the brain to find solutions we can't quite see. We seem to fall into food metaphors when describing this moment of the writing process: mentioning how we "stew" on our ideas or let them "marinate." The idea here is that, in the same way that a complex, flavorful broth develops slowly over time with no apparent outside intervention, the writer allows his mind to address the problem and make progress without conscious consideration. The happy result (often) of Incubation is Illumination—that "Aha" moment when we solve the puzzle.

Core Fear: Falling Too Far Behind

Incubation is particularly challenging because when we're in this stage, we can't see progress. Worse, we can't even see effort. And for a scholar facing a publication or promotion deadline, the idea that work is being done "behind the scenes" is not in the least bit soothing. Quite the opposite: the core fear that plagues us during Incubation is that if we don't keep hammering away at the problem, we will fall behind and never catch up. In addition, Incubating ideas can raise scholars' fears that they will never come back to work. This is especially the case for a scholar who has been caught in the cycle of procrastination and binging. When their experience with taking breaks is limited to the avoidance that's inherent to procrastination, it's easy to see why a short rest from regular writing might feel too risky. But even writers with a solid habit have experienced that mounting dread that comes at the end of winter break, when the thought of getting back to writing and classes seems impossible; or the exhaustion at the end of spring quarter when you need at least a month to recover from the previous year. In other words, worries about the difficulty of coming back after any kind of break are reasonable and partly based on the cycles of overwork built into scholarly life. It makes sense then that deliberately injecting *more* of these seemingly disruptive periods into your regular writing process might feel impossible.

Common Pitfall: Refusing to Stop

The pitfall scholars fall into in this case is pretty straightforward: they refuse to stop. They cannot bring themselves to willingly put down their work and "do nothing." Sure, we might procrastinate a little or accidentally stay longer at lunch than we meant to. Accidental breaks happen. However, I've yet to encounter more than a handful of scholars who are comfortable *deliberately* and *strategically* resting in order to solve a puzzle in their writing.

When we look at the science on rest, we see that such thinking is flawed. The quality of our work is dependent on our willingness to rest—and top performers in the arts, sports, and sciences are marked by the tendency to purposefully combine limited time in their practice with deliberate rest periods (Pang, 2016). In addition, we're more likely to have moments of epiphany when we've had a period of disengagement from our thinking (Kounios & Beeman, 2015). In other words, this strategy is so central to the cultivation of innovative ideas and problem-solving that it is worth taking the plunge and training ourselves to incubate early and often. But this is one arena in which, the science can say whatever it wants to. The strongest force in this instance is not science, but culture and consequences: specifically, the protestant work ethic that permeates Western culture as well as academia.[5] Combined with all the ways that Chapter 2 shows that writing is risky, refusing to stop seems like a very good idea to many, many scholars.

Essential Skill: Finding Rest Stops

One essential skill that we can develop to overcome the legitimate concerns and learned tendencies that lead to unceasing work, is to create Rest Stops in the middle of our writing. That is, to admit that we lack complete control over the process through which ideas formulate themselves in our minds. Instead, we can learn to actively hand that work over to time and our brain's unconscious processes and give ourselves a break from the work. Of course, disentangling effort from the outcome and relinquishing control over the pace of our work is anything but easy. But the rewards it offers to us and our writing are immense.

Try It Out: Finding Rest Stops

The first rung of Giving Up exercises includes specific writing-related tasks that feel like acceptable substitutes for the work of writing—so that you do not have to fully engage in the "nonwork" you may find challenging. The limitation of this set of activities is that they are less likely to lead to Illumination. However, they do the important work of giving the scholar's mind some form of rest and also making the habit palatable. I can't stress enough that these tasks are not the ideal forms of Incubation, because many do not encourage true rest. But they are nonetheless excellent strategies for working your way up to more restorative behavior.

The second rung of the Incubation ladder includes Rest Stops within your writing session: rest periods of two to ten minutes during which you place your attention on something other than your writing. The beauty of Rest Stops is that they do not require a lot of time, so they are an easy way to ease yourself into longer periods of Incubation. The reason these behaviors are so helpful is because they work *with* the brain instead of against it. The brain is actually built to be constantly scanning the environment for new and different stimuli. In particular, it's interested in whatever is changing or unexpected. So when we give the brain something different to pay attention to, we're capitulating to our biological tendencies, but doing so in a way that supports our capacity to solve our writing problems.

Tier I: Turning Away

Switching: Especially if you are someone who juggles multiple projects at once, switching between one writing project and another can give you a break without requiring you to "do nothing." Depending on how much time you have, you can switch within a single writing session or a single day (if you have multiple and lengthy writing blocks available). You can even concentrate on a project for a couple of weeks, then get to a good stopping point and work on another for the same period of time. While this strategy does not as strongly promote true Illumination, it does offer a break from the problems you're working on. All while allowing you to make a comfortable amount of progress on another project.

Chatting: Chatting includes any activities that pull you away from solo writing and put you in dialogue with others who are considering related ideas. We can think of it as a return to the Saturation stage—not to pad our literature review but to spark our imagination. Think: talks, stories, articles in *The New Yorker* and *The Root*, and documentaries that are tangential to your work. I especially find it useful to read the work of people who disagree with me politically, but are not hateful or disrespectful. This not only gives me a lens into a world I'm not familiar with, it also helps me humanize people I disagree with. And when the work is thoughtful, it helps me see the limitations of my own thinking and sharpen my arguments.

Admin: Another option is to use your time doing tasks that need to be done to make the writing easier, more efficient, and more likely to be completed on time but that do not involve difficult intellectual consideration that is especially fatiguing. Every publication involves these tasks, and they are essential. A sample list might include:

- Cleaning off your desk
- Organizing your electronic and hard copy files of articles and notes
- Organizing your books
- Throwing out material from previous projects
- Creating a note-taking system
- Creating a tagging system for your notes
- Creating or updating a project journal
- Finding, cleaning, and formatting citations
- Creating an image log
- Securing permissions for images

Tier II: Turning Off

Mind Wandering: Josh Davis suggests a helpful and research-backed strategy for deliberately resting your mind: "After focusing on a problem for a while, switch to a task that is mildly demanding from a cognitive standpoint—but one that doesn't require you to use your working memory—and then come back to the original problem you are trying to solve. Choose a task ahead of time, so you don't have to try to remember it once your mind has already started to wander" (2015, p. 87). Examples include:

- Appreciating nearby beauty (art, plants, windows)

- Neatening your space

- "Listening to music and noticing all the different instruments in the piece you are listening to" (2015, p. 88)

- "Playing a little game, such as making a mark on a piece of paper every time you see someone walking while texting" (2015, p. 88)

While I have primarily spoken of Incubation as a technique for helping move you past a stuck point in your writing process, this strategy has meaning well beyond what it can do for your prose. Incubation is the ultimate behavioral articulation of the power, freedom, and joy that lie at the heart of scholarly life. It is the exact and complete opposite of make work, which is labor that workers invent, engage in, and perform for their superiors in order to appear to be busy. Incubation, by contrast, is the purposeful disengagement from the active *obvious* labor of production, in acknowledgment of the equally active but *hidden* labor of discovery.

When we accept the need for Incubation, we are accepting the fact that the intellectual process is not completely within our control—that reasoned thinking and empirical analysis do not always take the mystery out of the world; rather, they both contain mysteries themselves. And when we move from acceptance to action and dive wholeheartedly into Incubation, we step, momentarily, just outside of the system that defines intellectual labor as useful only to the degree that it can produce a thing to be commodified. We step, instead, into a way of thinking about and interacting with our work that redefines that work as valuable in and of itself. This is no small thing. Because in taking this step, we risk being misinterpreted (that is, judged) as lazy or unproductive and losing the rewards of the profession. In Chapter 6, I discuss how we might join with others to make those risks more bearable and beneficial. For now, the small steps offered earlier allow you to experiment safely.

Clarification: Taking Your Ideas Out for a Test Run

Finally. The moment we've all been waiting for. The one when we are finally able to put our materials together in a way that looks like a manuscript. See here the full sentences that make sense. Observe there the quotations, citations, tables, and equations. Behold the paragraphs and arguments, all arranged in the proper order—one that leads the reader down a logical path that convinces them that what you're saying has merit. And right here? Here is a scholar who feels that, finally, for the first time, *she is writing*. But as I mention in Chapter 3, what distinguishes Clarification from the other stages of the writing process is not that it's the first moment that we're "writing," but that it's the first moment that we're primarily writing for others. It's at this point that we make three shifts in our focus: We change our

- **Audience**: Sharing our ideas with an imagined reader, and not just ourselves.

- **Purpose**: Communicating and explaining our thinking, instead of trying to uncover it.

- **Format**: Turning notes, charts, and outlines written for ourselves into paragraphs.

In short, we shift from explaining our ideas to ourselves in informal formats, to articulating and defending our ideas to others in formal formats.

Core Fear: Getting It Wrong

It's perfectly reasonable then, that at this stage, our primary concern is with "getting it right." And by "right" I mean, perfect the first time around. Given the substantial amount of work we've put into our writing, its meaning for our professional identity, and the high stakes involved, it's not surprising that at this stage, we are often desperate to make sure that our argument is impeccable. After so much hard work, we want to know exactly "what the book is about" even if we're not done collecting data. When someone asks what we're working on, we want that perfect thirty-second elevator pitch to describe what we're doing. We want the manuscript to fully and immediately reflect the complexity and sophistication we know the subject deserves, even though we're still in the middle of writing. Sometimes our fears during this phase are exacerbated by the work of other scholars, even—perhaps especially—those whose work we admire and want to emulate. With such admirable models and lofty goals for our work, it's understandable then, if our primary fear is that we will get it wrong.

Common Pitfall: Hiding Our Work

The pitfall we fall into at this stage is to hide our work. We refuse to share drafts with colleagues and advisors because we haven't yet gotten it "right." When we do present our work in public, we agonize over making a good impression with small portions of the project, devoting weeks and months to polishing them for public presentation, even when doing so requires us to sacrifice progress on the larger project of which they are a part. What makes hiding especially tricky is it often doesn't seem like hiding when we're doing it. Especially if our ideas are flowing relatively well, and the broad outlines of where we want to go are clear to us. It can seem like the work just "isn't ready yet," we just need a little more time before it's in good enough shape to get feedback. Sometimes this is true. And sometimes the "problems" we're trying to solve before sharing our work are just in need of a little outside input.

Essential Skill: Mocking Up Your Manuscript

To avoid this pitfall, we can Mock Up our ideas. The idea of the Mock Up comes from the design process, which emphasizes the importance of creating a rickety, real-life model of whatever you're creating, so that you can quickly see what works, what doesn't, and what needs to change.[6] Mocked Up manuscripts have four important characteristics. First, they are prepared relatively quickly. You don't spend months or years working out the idea. You just get it down on paper, because the purpose of the Mock Up is to illustrate arguments, not to insist on them. What are the flaws? Where are the holes? What things work and what things would we like to strengthen in the future? These are the questions that animate this phase of the writing process.

Part of the reason a manuscript Mock Up can be written so quickly is because of its second characteristic, which is that it is minimalist. Because its purpose is to help you see the overview of your thinking more clearly, it does not need to include every elaboration, disclaimer, exception, and subpoint. This feature is especially helpful for scholars who are stymied by the disappointment that their work is too simple and unsophisticated when they first put their ideas together. A quick and dirty presentation is the aim of the Mock Up—not a thorough elaboration.

Third, and perhaps most importantly for scholars who are using Mock Ups to move themselves past their fears, Mock Ups are *purposefully impermanent.* That is, they are designed not to be ground-breaking, field-defining interventions that will persist for years. Instead, they are *designed for destruction*—they're made with the flimsiest of materials (arguments and assertions) in order to give the writer an idea of what things could look like. Once the final product is finished, you may hang on to the Mock Up out of fondness or nostalgia. But ultimately, it is designed to be thrown away. Once it's shone a light on the next best direction of your project, its purpose is fulfilled, and it can easily be tossed.

Finally, and most importantly, Mock Ups are designed to elicit rapid, usable feedback. You write with your most important conversation partner in mind. But you do not write to *convince* them of anything. Instead, you write *to learn something from them.* In essence, a Mock Up is a draft with a narrow, specific purpose—not to be right, but to help you see things you couldn't see on your own.

Mocking Up is similar to Messing Up, in that both are designed to free us from the desire to make things absolutely perfect. The difference is that Messing Up involves making arguments, *to yourself,* that are deliberately wrong, in order to give you a starting point from which to move in the right direction. Mocking Up, on the other hand, involves making arguments, *to others,* that are deliberately right (or as right as we can make them), in order to make you aware of places where you're going in the wrong direction. Mock Ups are a great idea. But they are intimidating. How can you get yourself to make and share one if you are terrified of being criticized? Here are four powerful strategies for doing so.

Try It Out: How to Mock Up Your Manuscript

Remember, these exercises are designed, not just to build your tolerance for sharing imperfect work, but to also help you hone in on your argument—or, what ScholarShape founder Margy Thomas calls your Story-Argument.[7] Thomas describes scholarly writing as a process of both discovery and invention, one where storytelling and argumentation fuse together to create meaning. For Thomas, the long process of determining our Story-Argument is akin to fumbling with a large ring of keys. Each of these keys is a working thesis. A hint at a "revelation." A "provisional claim that . . . may turn out to be the one essential idea." What's particularly useful about Thomas's notion of this process is how she describes the moment when we hit the one true idea: "The knob turns in your hand, the door gives way, and finally you can see in one sweeping glance *what previously you had only been glimpsing in patches under doors or through windows.*"[8]

Before encountering Thomas's take on this moment of the writing process, I'd drafted sections of this chapter that conceived of writing as a series of "constant failures." Doing so was my attempt to normalize the fact that writing is inherently difficult, and that part of the work involved in drafting is bearing the disappointment that comes from sharing imperfect work. But Thomas's conception of at first seeing only *glimpses* of our idea zeroes in more precisely on the true nature of what's really happening. It's not that what we're doing when constructing Story-Arguments is right or wrong. It's that all our efforts up until that moment are both right *and* wrong. Because they are *partial* visions of exactly the right thing. When you Mock Up your manuscript, you ask other people to look through those doors and windows with you and tell you what they see. Doing so helps you move more quickly from partial visions to entire vistas.

Tier I: Mock Up With Your Mouth

Back Talk

Sometimes the best feedback comes from yourself. If you're trying to figure something out but having a hard time making sense of it on paper, try capturing your ideas in some other medium besides text. Turn on your phone's voice recorder and say out loud what you've been thinking; collect images that represent what you're trying to capture—you can sketch, create a Pinterest board, or make a hard copy collage. Use physical objects (children's toys are great, as are knickknacks, and kitchen supplies) to represent concepts and move them around to illustrate the relationships you see. Once you're done, free-write about what you've expressed.

The Back & Forth

Let's say you feel pretty comfortable sharing and getting feedback on imperfect work but don't want to take the time to write it down, even in bullets or mind maps. Maybe you don't even know what feedback you need. One of the easiest ways to figure it out is to simply have a conversation. Ask a friend, loved one, or colleague for thirty minutes of their time and record your conversation about what's going on with your project. To give the conversation some structure, tell them (1) what you're working on and (2) what's giving you so much trouble. Recording the conversation allows the back and forth to be as natural as possible, and still lets you mine the good parts once it's over.

The Brain Dump

If your conversation partner is willing, try an even better version of *The Back & Forth*, which I learned from writer and audio producer Heather Radke. She calls it the *Brain Dump*: "I just say everything I'm thinking about an essay or whatever into a memo and then [my partner] listens and asks me questions about it and we go back and forth, and I refine and articulate the idea that way. I find it so helpful. [It's] low stakes. I feel like I'm kind of tricking myself into doing some of the work when I feel stuck."[9] The beauty of the *Brain Dump* is that it's not really a brain dump at all. It might start that way, but as you proceed through the conversation, you're able to clarify the parts of your argument, identify holes, and also get more clear about what you mean, all in an environment that is encouraging rather than demeaning or destructive.

Tier II: Mock Up in Your Manuscript

The "No Bad News" Writing Group[10]

In a No Bad News (NBN) writing group, you exchange short (two to four page) Mock Ups with one or more people on a regular schedule. In turn, each member of the group gives and gets feedback on the pages they've submitted. But the feedback is minimal. It consists of a checkmark that indicates which parts of the manuscript the reader found especially compelling and would like to see more of. No comments. No questions. No requests for clarification. Just unrelenting support for what is working, so you can find some hope and motivation to keep writing. NBN Writing Groups are easy, and effective, and anyone can do them. They're easy to both set up and maintain, because they don't require a lot of people. Nor do they require a lot *from* people. They offer accountability and encouragement without requiring a weekly meeting. And they're great at helping shy scholars get in the habit of writing quickly and sharing their work before they think it's ready—instead of getting hung up on its imperfections.

Tier III: The "Mean Ole Lion" Writing Group[11]

Once you've built trust with a group of people and gotten the hang of sharing imperfect work, experiment with receiving feedback that is both more substantive and critical. Exchange the same number of pages as you do in the "No Bad News" Writing Group. But instead of offering content-empty checkmarks, each reader will choose *one* place in the manuscript where they answer the question: "What don't you understand?" This question has many benefits as a feedback prompt, and it's worth discussing those benefits with the other group members, to make sure everyone's on the same page.[12] It elicits precision about the limitations of the manuscript, in language that helps the writer see more clearly how our language and logic choices impact the reader. And it does this by providing the writer with one single issue they can examine and address.

Submission: Leading Yourself to Release

Submission is a moment in the writing process that's not prominently featured in conventional theories and descriptions of the creative process (Tharp & Reiter, 2003; Bane, 2012; Evans, 2013). It tends to be incorporated into Hibernation and therefore glossed over. But I have separated it from that moment for several reasons. The first is that this phase involves a kind of hidden work that, if we are not aware of it, can sour the joys of having finally completed a manuscript. When we don't account for that work, it's easy to miss deadlines or be forced to cram that work in at the last minute in order to finish the manuscript on time. When that happens, the natural crunch period of finishing a project becomes even more hurried and intense. Our manuscripts sometimes end up with ragged edges, despite our having worked so long and hard to get them done. In fact, it was my own struggle with the hidden work of Submission that first led me to think through the importance of the writing metaphor for scholars (Boyd, 2012).

A second reason I distinguish Submission from Hibernation is because fear of this moment is one of the sharpest I see among scholars. At its best, fear of Submission prevents us from hitting send until the very last minute: we fiddle with manuscripts as long as we can, then work in a mad rush to get them in before the deadline. At its worst, fear of Submission prevents us from hitting send at all—it lies at the root of much Endless Writing. And there is nothing more disheartening than a scholar with a book that everyone can see is brilliant, who fails to get tenure because they never really believe the manuscript is "ready."

And yet, as Mike Sharples points out to us, this inability to see a piece of writing as truly finished is in some ways baked into the nature of writing itself. He argues that writing is a kind of design process and that no designer ever feels their work is completely finished:

> It follows that a designer is rarely pleased with the product, but stops when it no longer seems worth the effort of trying to improve its quality, or when halted by some external factor such as running out of time and resources. What a designer intends can never be rendered exactly. The more original the message, the more a designer has a feeling of having inadequately

expressed it. "That is why it is dangerous to let an author correct his own proofs; he always wants to rewrite the book." (Sharples, 1999, p. 61)

It's easy to judge someone who has trouble letting their work go, to scoff at them for allowing their fears to overcome them when it seems so obvious to us that the work is more than good enough. But the truth is, many of us do this with something in our lives. And many of us do it with our writing in less extreme ways. We don't tell our advisors our thoughts about the dissertation, because we're afraid they're not good enough. We ask for incompletes in grad classes and extensions from editors and discussants because we can't bear the idea of sharing our messy, confused drafts. We don't get feedback while writing because we can't identify someone who really "gets" our work well enough for us to share it with them—these are all mini versions of this same behavior: avoiding the moment of exposure for as long as we can.

Core Fear: Being Found Out

It's this fear of finally being *exposed*, in all our imperfections, that prevents many scholars from submitting our work. In some ways, this is similar to the fear we face in the Clarification stage—a looming certainty that we won't get things "right" and an attendant unwillingness to therefore put ideas down on paper. But here, at the moment of Submission, we face a more particular version of that fear. In my experience, it's not just that scholars are afraid of being criticized once they publish their work. What we're truly afraid of is that the criticism will lead to being found out. As a fraud, as unworthy, as not really a (enter your discipline here). Public exposure to our work opens us up to all manner of challenges. And once something is in print, it's not just our ideas that are on display: *we* are on display. With all our faults and inadequacies. Submission is the moment most obviously related to the feeling that we are imposters, and this is going to be the moment we're finally found out. What keeps us from moving forward at this point is not just our desire to be perfect, but the inability to normalize imperfection. That is, we mistakenly believe that the route to finishing is to finally make the work as strong as it should be. This translates into a dogged commitment to "improving" the work even though we've been given multiple, clear signals that the time for improving the work is over.

Essential Skill: Patch Up and Let Go

Instead of continuing to improve the work, we need, instead, to actively and purposefully *release* the manuscript by Patching it Up and letting it go. I'm not saying we need to make a single decision and "send it off already." Instead, I'm suggesting that we need to deliberately walk ourselves through a process of facing, mourning, and letting go of our ideal manuscript. To gradually prepare both the manuscript and ourselves for the moment when we have to let it go, even though there are so many more things we could do, if we just had the time. This process of mourning our ideal manuscript and accepting our real manuscript is one we go through at some point whenever we send it off to others. It's just that we often wait until the last minute: rushing through it once the deadline has arrived and forcing ourselves through it. The work of Patching Up is merely reckoning with that process earlier and more deliberately than we might otherwise do.

The manuscript problems I'm suggesting we accept are not ethical lapses in the gathering, analysis, or representation of the data. Nor are they outsized claims based on the data we do have available. Instead, I'm referring here to omissions in the exploration of ideas and weaknesses in the development of our arguments. We wanted to discuss a book that just came out about our topic to make sure we're showing the relevance of our writing to the most recent debates. We make a claim in Chapter 2 that needs a little more support and we haven't had time (or figured out how) to elucidate why this claim still makes sense. We used so-and-so's conceptual framework to illuminate the phenomenon we observed and were never quite satisfied with their terminology— but have yet to find language that more accurately encapsulates our thinking. These are the kinds of intellectual moves we may desperately wish to make, ones that fit our ideal notion of how magnificent this manuscript was going to be when we first hatched the idea. This ideal notion is one we often must release if we ever want the work to see the light of day. To let go of these ideal notions—to avoid the pitfall of refusing to submit our work, we can go from perfecting our work to Patching Up our work.

I'll be honest: when I first developed the Patching strategy, I called it "Papering Over Your S**t." I used this more straightforward, and . . . informal phrasing to press my coaching clients into recognizing three things: first, that all of us have portions of manuscripts we're dissatisfied with; second, that all of us, at one time or another, have decided to submit those imperfect manuscripts anyway; and third, that all of us, whether conscious of it or not, do that by accepting those problems instead of resolving them. I intended to illustrate that our decisions about our work are always impacted by external resources of time and energy, and to emphasize: there's no shame in that.

Yet, as I've thought more about this strategy, I realized that the original phrasing, though much more fun, was not as accurate as Patching Up. The concept of Papering Over suggests that all we're doing when submitting the manuscript is sneakily obscuring something shameful. The wording itself has the potential to amplify a scholar's fear of exposure by suggesting that they're doing something inappropriate. Most importantly, the idea of Papering Over inadvertently validates the idea that an argument that has weak points has no value at all, and that the scholar must first hide that weakness, and then hide the hiding. Not only does this exacerbate the problem of Endless Writing, but it is contrary to the spirit behind intellectual inquiry—which calls upon us to publicly admit the limitations of our findings in order to strengthen the body of knowledge available to all and point other scholars toward future research topics.

The concept of Patching Up, on the other hand, highlights the fact that we do not need to eliminate every weakness in our manuscript in order for it to be ready for Submission. Nor do we need to hide those weaknesses. Instead, we can Patch Up the work—that is, we can mend or strengthen a manuscript's weak points to make the whole stronger.[13] When we patch clothing, we place a small piece of material over a hole or area that's grown thin in order to keep it from fraying, growing larger, and making the object unwearable. Similarly, when we patch an argument, we place intellectual material and argumentative moves over the gaps and weak points in our manuscript. We do this both to keep them from growing and to ensure the integrity of the rest of the argument. In other words, we make the weaker portions of the work tolerable in a way that thereby actually strengthens the whole manuscript. We do that to *prioritize its submission*—a choice that is both practical and honorable.

An important thing to note about patches is that they aren't sneaky. They're obvious—clearly distinguishable from the rest of the argument. They are some-times temporary—put in place until a stronger, more long-term option can be implemented. But they are often permanent, as uncomfortable as that may be. So, patches are appropriate for early and intermediate feedback requests as well as final submissions.

The concept of Patching Up also emphasizes the fact that we must go through a *process* in order to stop trying to perfect the work. Without a pressing deadline, merely insisting that we "need to stop" often won't work. And even with a deadline on the horizon, we will often spend so much time trying to eliminate imperfect bits that the process of submission becomes immobilizing, then painfully rushed. We need, instead, to first acknowledge that we're in the moment of Submission. Then, we need to use it to walk ourselves through the emotional and intellectual process of accepting our manuscript's imperfections.

Try It Out: Patching Up

To do that, we must release our vision of what the manuscript "could have" or "should have" been and redirect our efforts toward strengthening what exists. How do we do that? We look squarely at the manuscript's limitations, and we admit them (find, mark, and name the hole); we accept them (measure, choose, and apply the patch); and we account for them (smooth the edges). Here's what that might look like:

1. **Find and Mark the Hole.** Sometimes we know exactly what the problem is when we're unhappy with our work—a list of issues we've been able to ignore, only because we promised ourselves that we could address them while revising. Other times we have a vague sense that what we've done isn't right—a hazy memory from several months prior, when we last worked on a chapter, that it needed fixing. Regardless of the source of the criticism, your first task is to merely note in the manuscript where you or someone else has indicated that something is amiss—without specifying the nature of the omission.

2. **Name the Hole.** Step two is to specify exactly what *you* think is missing from the work—and *write it down*. Making a list of the relevant issues converts what may be a vague and fearful sense of dissatisfaction into an actionable and manageable to-do list. In addition, it allows you to practice an underrated, but important part of the submission

process—deciding which of the reviewer's comments you agree with and want to respond to. Novice writers tend to assume that they are obligated to address all of the issues mentioned by reviewers, whether they agree with them or not. Naming the Hole is partly about clarifying what the manuscript needs. But it's also about exercising your authority as an author.

3. **Measure the Holes.** Next, you want to specify what kind of work needs to be done to eliminate or "fill" each hole. In other words, in an ideal world, if you were able to address this problem to your complete satisfaction, what would you do? Here are some of the more common types of work:

> **Discovery** is work that requires uncovering additional information. Examples include doing an additional reading to make sure your manuscript speaks to the very latest work in the field, gathering additional data, or conducting additional analyses to confirm your findings.

> **Puzzling** involves working through and finding answers to unanswered questions. It can be theoretical or empirical—that is, it may or may not involve Discovery. In short, puzzling is an attempt to come up with solutions to thorny problems.

> **Elaboration** includes efforts to deepen your arguments or illuminate their complexity in ways you know would be helpful but *have not yet thought through*. Like Puzzling, Elaboration requires significant mental processing of ideas. But it differs from Puzzling in that it is not unclear or mysterious. It could be completed if you had adequate time to acquire or review the ideas and think through their complexities and associations with one another.

> **Specification** is making something you already understand clearer, more explicit, or more precise. When we articulate previously unspoken assumptions, define terms, specify causal actors and mechanisms, or more precisely state relationships, we are engaged in the work of Specification. The key difference between this and the previous three categories of work is that Specification does not require you to obtain (from others) or discover (for yourself) any new information or greater clarity. The specification can be accomplished with information you already have at your cognitive fingertips. It may be aided by references and review but does not require them.

> **Attribution** is the worst, isn't it? Now we must manage all those citations, hastily scribbled and carelessly filed, in digital or analog

format, in various locations. Attribution involves the painstaking work of finding and including all the details of the bibliographic and citation information that you need. It also includes the administrative and relational work needed to secure permissions.

Formatting includes copyediting and any other work involved in meeting requirements about the arrangement and presentation of text and images in the manuscript, such as margins, titles, headers, citations, charts, tables, and photographs.

I hope it is obvious that the first half of this list—Discovery, Solving, and Elaboration—are the work of *revision,* the moment when we are still refining our ideas. Specification, Attribution, and Formatting are what we should be doing when we have reached the moment of *Submission.* If we are trying to do anything else, then we have not truly accepted the painful reality of the moment. This makes sense. When we're in a breathless race to perfect a manuscript, we can be overwhelmed by our sense that the work is inadequate, and have little desire or ability to think through the scope and the depth of what we're asking of ourselves. Facing this reality is the purpose of Measuring the Hole. Recognizing the possibilities in this reality is the purpose of the next step.

4. **Choose Your Patch.** Now that you have identified what's missing, where it's located, and what you wish you could do about it, you want to deliberately choose an *alternate* method of addressing whatever problem you've identified. Your aim here is not to eliminate the weakness you've identified by generating new work. Instead, you aim to compensate for the weakness, by choosing a strategy that strengthens what your manuscript does well, that reinforces the quality of what's already there. If your manuscript were a pair of jeans with a hole in the knee, you would not be going out and buying a new pair of jeans. You'd be finding a patch to place over the hole at the knee so that you can go out in public without worry or shame. Patches can vary and may include the following:

   a. **Ignore** Intentionally choose *not* to address an issue.

   b. **Delete** Eliminate passages that raise the issue you are unable to address.

   c. **Gesture** Raise and refer to the desired subject broadly and briefly. Works well with Narrowing and Redirecting.

   d. **Narrow** State explicitly that the unexplored issue is beyond the scope of the present work but addresses one small dimension that requires only specification work.

   e. **Redirect** Point to other work—your own (existing or forthcoming) or others'—that addresses the point in question.[14]

     f.   **Speculate** Leave the material to the conclusion or implications sections, the scholar's version of the Land of Misfit Toys. Here you have license to briefly address omitted material by exploring possible conclusions, imagining possibilities, and suggesting future research questions.

5.   **Apply the Patch.** Now that you have made a clear distinction between what might have been and what is actually possible, it's time to get down to the work of finishing and submitting. Go through each hole in your manuscript, and choose the alternative response that you have already identified. It seems like the main work you're doing here is intellectual. But in fact, the emotional work you're doing is just as important. You may be uncomfortable the entire time you are doing this work. You may feel sad, frustrated, and worried to be Patching instead of perfecting. You may feel a strange mix of deflated exhilaration, as you experience the paradox that the more you let go of trying to improve the manuscript, the closer you get to submitting it. *Your primary goal in this stage is to feel your feelings, and keep Patching anyway.* That's because Patching is a strangely contradictory act. It's a moment of both mourning and making—when we let our hoped-for manuscript die so that our real manuscript—the one that actually exists—can live.

6.   **Smooth the Edges.** Even if you feel some relief or pleasure from having readied the manuscript for Submission, it's normal to also feel trepidation about sharing this altered version with the world. That's why this last step in the Submission process is to smooth the edges of the patch by framing your work—that is, to direct the reviewer's attention toward the choices you've made, the resulting revisions you've made, and their significance for the manuscript. When we frame the work, we don't pretend that its limitations don't exist, and we don't exaggerate its strong points. Rather, we select a few strengths and limitations from the long list of each and create a clear narrative about the piece that helps the reader understand its value. We typically think of framing as something we do for the external reader—a way of setting their expectations so they know what's coming. However, especially in the final moment of Submission, framing can be as significant for the author as it is for the reader. To frame your work, introduce your manuscript to your reader by answering three basic questions:

     a.   What assertions or revisions does the manuscript make?

     b.   What issues does the manuscript *not* address?

     c.   Why do your changes make sense? In other words, how do they improve the argument?

Hibernation: Immersion in Play, Not Work

Hibernation takes place at the end of a project, when you deliberately turn from active, intense writing to rest and restoration. It's a pause in the writer's work life, designed to give your mind, body, and spirit time to restore the resources you used in completing the writing project. Or at least it should be. In reality, it's often difficult to take this stage seriously, given the excessive demands for publication, the backlog of projects we may have, or the personal responsibilities that have been ignored as we finished the manuscript.

Core Fear: That Just Can't Happen

Unlike other stages of the writing process, the idea of Hibernation evokes not just fear, but outright refusal. When I mention to coaching clients that the solution to their inability to write might be to take even a short break, the most common responses I receive are laughter and irritation—quickly followed by shock when they realize I am serious. The idea seems so ridiculous that many scholars honestly cannot imagine a way that true rest could actually take place. On rare occasions, the scholar will consent to take off a couple of days—maybe a three-day weekend if they're feeling adventurous. But generally, my insistence that rest is a natural and *necessary* phase of writing is seen as delusional. And it certainly isn't legitimate.

This is a shame, because the many natural pauses built into the academic year are perfect for practicing such breaks. They provide natural openings for reigniting our enthusiasm for our work. Because the idea seems so ludicrous to us, the pitfall that many scholars fall into is that, when we reach the Hibernation phase of our writing project—or when we reach one of the natural moments in the year when we could take any kind of break—we instead choose to work through them, using them to catch up on the backlog of work created when we focus primarily on one project. The weeks off for spring and fall break; reading week; the time between finals and the start of the next semester; the four-day weekend that surrounds Thanksgiving in the United States—these moments of potential rest either whiz by in a fury of grading, or are commonly viewed as the best time to "get some writing done."

This wasn't always the case. Eells points out that, although they didn't use the term then, in the late nineteenth and early twentieth centuries, sabbaticals were widely understood as a form of Hibernation. He points to a 1907 report from Columbia University's Board of Trustees that asserted that sabbaticals are fundamental to intellectual life. Why? Because "university teaching must be progressive; it requires on the part of the teaching body, as it were, a periodical refurbishing of its equipment" (Eells, 1962, p. 253).[15] Even more significantly, the committee argued that paying faculty members during this period of "refurbishment" was a requirement, because connecting with other institutions, scholars, and methods is "an intellectual and practical necessity . . .

which cannot be obtained during the summer vacation, as this is a period of rest practically everywhere" (italics mine). In other words, sabbaticals evolved, not only because universities recognized the value of giving faculty members time to refresh their professional connections. It evolved because universities recognized rest during summer break as a legitimate activity for scholars that should not be infringed upon.

Since then, both summer and sabbatical have changed. Summer has been transformed from a period of rejuvenation and refreshment to its very opposite: one in which scholars seek to be *especially* productive. And as Max Page argues in his essay "Who Took the Sabbath out of Sabbatical?" sabbatical has gone from being a period in which scholars built their connections and capacity to one in which they up their output (2010). In short, the difficulty scholars have resting is a direct result of academic work intensification and the notion that the route to the highest quality scholarship is to work all the time.

Essential Skill: Take a Deep Dive Into Delight

One way to push past cultural norms and professional expectations against Hibernation is to practice doing Deep Dives: to immerse yourself so completely in your restorative activity that writing is either impossible or highly unattractive. The idea isn't to "do nothing" or try to "just relax" during that time. Exhortations to relax more aren't especially effective against the cultural and institutional pressures that encourage overwork and suggest that scholars who are not working are lazy (Shahjahan, 2014).

Doing a Deep Dive means fully hooking into something so engrossing that you seduce yourself away from work. When Hibernation is this enthralling, it not only becomes something to look forward to as you're finishing the previous project; it also provides the kind of restoration of energy and enthusiasm that Hibernation is meant to. Scholars who study rest show that the best kinds of activities to engage in are those that are startlingly similar to the Flow experience we seek as writers. Like writing flow, truly restorative activities involve a clear sense of control—you have the autonomy to decide when and what to do. They often involve efforts at mastery—some activity that is *just* challenging enough to be interesting without being demoralizing. Ideal rest periods also involve the same mental detachment we find in writing flow. We become unaware of and disconnected from our immediate surroundings as well as our worries and fears because we're so deeply engaged in what we're doing (Pang, 2016). How do Deep Dives *differ* from writing flow? One core difference is that they involve relaxation. They are pleasant, undemanding, and reduce the tension and anxiety we feel about work.

Try It Out: Deep Diving

For most scholars I work with, Deep Diving is incredibly difficult—until it isn't. What I mean is that the beginning steps are the ones that seem the most outrageous and incomprehensible. But getting started helps to chip away at the sense that rest is impossible. So, even more than is the case with other phases of the writing process, it pays to start small by dipping your toe in the water. To temporarily replace the all-consuming act of writing with an activity that's equally consuming, but much more restorative, we can look to the winter-time responses of flora and fauna for useful models.

Tier I: Preparing to Dive In

Store Up Resources: To make the idea of Hibernation more palatable, it helps to begin thinking and planning for it before the time comes. Specifically, begin gathering the resources you'll need for your Deep Dive, whatever it will be. Many of us are familiar with childhood images of squirrels fattening up in late fall, storing away nuts in tree hollows so they can survive the long winter. Similarly, scholars can begin collecting and saving the materials that will make their Hibernation more attractive leading up to it, and more effective while in the midst of it. The word "resources" may seem to be a sly way of mentioning money, especially if your Hibernation period is going to overlap with a sabbatical. But the most important resources are not financial in a Hibernation: they are the materials that will allow you to fully sink into the experience. Imagine, for example, a Hibernation in which you long to clean your office and get rid of the syllabi and class notes from your undergraduate or graduate school classes. Perhaps you need to collect green cleaning supplies. Or start saving boxes every time you get something delivered. The idea here is partly about getting the materials. But it's also about building your excitement for the Hibernation itself. Maybe you're a social scientist who's decided you will spend a month reading novels; or a lit scholar who's going to binge-watch nature documentaries. Start making lists, downloading books, saving URLs. Have you decided you're going to spend a couple of weeks golfing? Start booking your tee times and somebody to watch your kids. Then negotiate with your partner so you can have the car for those two weeks. The idea here is to think about what you will need to have your time away, and start getting it in place. Doing so creates momentum that's easier to follow once the time comes.

Abscise. Abscission is what happens when trees drop their leaves in anticipation of colder weather. We tend to think of fall leaves dropping on the ground as a sign that the tree is "dying." In fact, trees drop leaves because leaves require so much energy to feed and maintain. And with cold temperatures and less sunlight on the way, trees need to preserve the little energy they'll have to maintain the roots, trunk, and branches of the tree—the essential parts that contain the mechanisms of communication and nutrient absorption. Similarly, when we're in a writing Hibernation, it's helpful to think about what obligations we can afford to set aside temporarily, so that we can fully detach from our writing.

Is it possible for you to skip out on talks being given by your colleagues? If your work is linked to current events, can you bypass the news for a while? If you're Hibernating in your office, can you put away the papers and books that are linked to the project you'll be finishing? Much of what we do each day is a function of routine and the sense that "it's expected." Consider what parts of your day can be released—just for a short while—then let people know you won't be available ahead of time, so they'll expect less from you during your planned Hibernation.

Migrate: Not a necessity, but certainly a boon. If you can go someplace else, even for a short period you will find that it's much easier to fully detach. If resources are tight, migration can be as simple as spending time outside your office (can you Hibernate at a café in a neighborhood whose primary language is not your own? Can you stay at a friend's place? Rent an Airbnb?) or working in a different medium (reading print newspapers instead of digital—if you can find them). The idea here is to make a shift in your context, one that for you feels like moving to a different world.

Tier II: Test Out the Waters

How long should your Hibernation last? Ideally, as long as it takes to feel energetic and enthusiastic about your writing again. Easy to say, but we often don't know exactly how long that will be. So one way you might calculate it is to use the length of your Summer Slump as a barometer. Think about that period—sometime in May or June—when grades are finally in, you don't have to think about prepping class for months and, against your every intention, you end up in a Netflix stupor while trying to muster up some energy to work. However long that lasts is probably a good length of time for your Hibernation.

Even if we do have a sense of how long the ideal Hibernation might be, it may feel daunting to think about taking a long break from writing. Especially if the teaching term's in full swing, or you're a junior scholar concerned with reputation management (see Chapter 2). If that's the case, then it helps to start with Hibernation periods that are short and intense and then build up to longer ones. Obviously, shorter periods will not be sufficient to fully restore you. But they can at least act as a moment of recognition and celebration of your completed project. And you can use them as practice—stepping-stones to longer periods of Hibernation you can engage in once you feel more comfortable. Consider the following options:

Lunchtime Hibernation (two hours): Set aside two hours for a long lunch at your favorite restaurant or a takeout feast. Order one of everything you love and plan for leftovers. During your meal, chew slowly and mindfully, delighting in the experience of the food with all five senses. Don't forget dessert. After you're done with your meal, reflect on all the work you put into your manuscript and how it feels to finally be done.

If, like me, you're a fan of dining alone, bring a journal and write these things down. You might also consider lunching with a supportive colleague or loved one, letting them know that the express intent of this lunch is to take a deliberate, restorative, celebratory break from writing before turning to your next project. No shoptalk allowed, other than the recognition of all you've accomplished. And how fabulous the food is.

Flaneur Hibernation (six hours): Pick a day when you're not teaching and walk around a part of town you don't normally spend time in. You can spend the whole day walking, dipping into cafés, public libraries, and shops. If it's cold or you dislike the outdoors, move your stroll indoors and hop from place to place. Museums and galleries that fix your attention on visuals (rather than text) are perfect. If you've done all the downtown galleries, find some neighborhood gems like thrift stores, antique stores, open markets, or musical performances. Anything that deeply engages your senses.

Day Tripping Hibernation (twelve hours): If you're feeling especially adventurous, spend the entire day, sunup to sundown, far away from where you spend most of your time. Take a day trip to a state park: sleep in, drive or take the train, hike all day and eat all your meals out of town, and don't come home until well after dinner. Take a yoga or meditation retreat in the next town over. Cross state lines and check out a historic house or a mountain bike trail you've been meaning to get to. It doesn't matter what you do—the idea is to get far away from everyday life for a full, pleasantly tiring day.

Hobby Hibernation. I am obsessed with tiny things—dollhouses, Lego models, Tiny Kitchen—how about you? Spend the weekend geeking out on your favorite non-text-related hobby. Knitting, woodworking, gardening, sewing, photography, bird-watching, cooking, baking, origami, coloring, weaving, embroidery, calligraphy, camping, brewing beer, crafting cocktails, puzzles (jigsaw, escape room, crossword, or Sudoku), video or board games, juggling, stamp collecting, parachuting, bungee jumping, pottery . . . You get the idea. Each of these activities could take an hour or a lifetime. If you don't have a hobby, grab a friend and try one out. Even better, pick the one you think you won't like and see what happens.

Conclusion

Figuring out our writing process is a lifelong pursuit. I for one, long for certainty and comfort in writing—for the day when I'll know exactly what to do and be able to dive in, headlong, with no hesitations. What I've found instead, is that writing is not a certainty, it's a mystery—in both senses of the word: It is an experience that feels unknowable. At the same time, writing is a puzzle to be solved. I've tried, in this chapter, to acknowledge both aspects of the mystery of writing. The strategies here do not provide definitive answers; instead, they offer possible paths. That means we have to recognize that the time we spend writing is not just a moment for production. It is also a moment for growth—a time when we must give at least some of our attention to sharpening our tools and honing our technique. So that we can remember who we are as writers and recover the pleasures and satisfactions of the work. Up until now, we've focused on the interior work we can do to reconnect with our writing process. Yet, that work is more powerful if we do it in community with others. Chapter 6 explores how we can do that.

Notes

1. A very mundane example of this is how difficult it is for some people to free-write since free-writing requires turning on a spigot that releases a flood of irrelevant, unclear, poorly considered, ill defended ideas.

2. Thanks to Liz Emens of Columbia University for introducing me to the concept and to Barry Saltzman's children's book of the same name.

3. The literature review is the most stripped-down expression of the Saturation moment in the writing process. But even when we are collecting data, we are still in Saturation—it's just that the information we're steeping ourselves in is information that we ourselves are uncovering.

4. It doesn't help that the people we most admire, our mentors and advisors and intellectual heroes, seem to have an encyclopedic knowledge of multiple bodies of work. Rather than understand that as the result of a long career, we take it as a mastery we need to achieve immediately.

5. As Kathi Weeks points out, the problem with the protestant work ethic is not just its valorization of work, but the way it defines work and hard work at that as the determinant of our moral worth (Weeks, 2011).

6. Thanks to my niece Sidney Stevens for making me aware of this strategy while pursuing an undergraduate degree in mechanical engineering. This concept also dovetails nicely with Tara Mohr's concept of Leaping, which she describes in her book *Playing Big* (2014).

7. Personal communication.

8. Personal communication.

9. Personal Communication, April 27, 2020.

10. In honor of Evileen from *The Wiz*. And thanks to Louise Seamster for inspiring this idea in her June 15, 2017, Chronicle Vitae article

"Why You Need a Writing Group." Now Available in the Chronicle Productivity Guide to Writing & Publishing https://hhs.uncg.edu/office-of-research/wp-content/uploads/sites/5/2022/02/The-Chronicle-Productivity-Guide-to-Writing-Publishing.pdf.

11. In honor of the Cowardly Lion, also from *The Wiz*, whose roar was much worse than his bite.

12. The benefits of giving and receiving feedback in response to this prompt are significant: First, it is familiar to every professor who's faced a room (or screen) full of silent students, run to the library seeking strategies to boost classroom engagement, and run across this suggestion for generating responses. Adopting the language that we use with our students highlights the fact that the feedback moment is a *learning* moment—regardless of who you are. As such, this moment requires the same care and precision that we would use with any person who is taking a risk by exposing what they know and do not know to someone else. The second benefit of this question is that it steers even the most thoughtless responder away from the judgmental, personalized, yet vague language that plagues many instances of feedback (e.g., "This doesn't make sense," or "What's your point here????"). Instead, it pushes the reader to respond to the manuscript by highlighting their *own* experience with it—what *they* do not understand, as opposed to what is *wrong* with the manuscript or the author.

13. Contrast this to what we typically try to do, which is Knit Up an argument. When knitters find a hole in our stitches, we move back to the original place the mistake began and catch up on whatever dropped stitches we missed. In the end, no one but the knitter is even aware that "mistakes were made," because they have been eliminated. A commitment to Knitting Up our manuscript is appropriate during the revision process, but it is disastrous at the moment of Submission.

14. Haven't yet drafted the piece you're imagining will address the issues? Throw all the ideas you've had to leave out in a new document. It is now a Work in Progress. Not only is this an accurate statement of the state of the manuscript, but it is also a fair and accurate admission of the state of your *ideas*. Nascent, yes. Undeveloped, yes. But still yours.

15. Even more significant was the understanding that the well-being of the institution and that of the individual were linked, that scholars served their institution by taking breaks so that sabbatical "was established not in the interests of the professors themselves *but for the good of university education*" (Eells, 1962, p. 253).

Thoughts on Building
a Writing Life

"In 1989, a reporter for The Sun knocked on Tyler's door and told her she had won the Pulitzer Prize for fiction for 'Breathing Lessons.' 'I'm in the middle of writing a sentence, so I can't be interrupted,' Tyler said as she shut the door, 'but I'm very pleased.'"

–Mary Carole McCauley[1]

When I finish teaching this material to scholars, I typically see three reactions from them. The first is relief: They finally understand what gets in the way of their writing—and are wowed by the idea that they're not the problem. The second reaction is hope. They have a budding sense that they can overcome the barriers that have stymied them for so long. Even if they don't know all of them or aren't sure if they'll work every time. That doesn't kill their hope, because the previously amorphous problems they've been facing are now nameable. They can be categorized and assessed, studied and managed. The writing metaphor has turned their shapeless, foggy fear into a precise and manageable problem.

The final reaction? Doubt. Maybe you're feeling some of that yourself. How on earth will you find the time and space to try these solutions out? Maybe you're too tired to even try, with all you have going on. And if you do get the time, how will you find the focus and courage to pursue these strategies? After a recent workshop on the Writing Metaphor, one scholar voiced the fears of many others: "This was great," she said, "But how can we do these things given the context of our everyday lives?" In that workshop, I hadn't even touched on how academia's work expectations and professional culture negatively impact our ability to write. And yet, the fact of those realities hung in the air, tinging each scholar's sense of possibility, shaking their confidence in their new insights, and causing them to wonder: is it even possible to create the conditions we need in order to follow our own writing process?

Making Space for Yourself and Your Writing

There are two ways to ask this question. One way is to ask a life-hacking question, to ask: what efficiencies and technologies can we implement to manage the ever-increasing onslaught of demands that make it difficult to write? This version of the question rests on the idea that, while the situation is grave, it can eventually be managed by the correct combination of planning systems, to-do lists, and internet blockers. Do you schedule your writing? Do you have a task-management system? How effective are you at ignoring email? This approach aims to help scholars thrive in an admittedly imperfect system, with the hope that, once they reach a certain level of security, comfort, and prestige, they can loosen their grip on these time-management and self-regulation routines, returning when it is safe to a looser and more loving relationship with their writing.

It's impossible to be an academic writing coach without sometimes relying on the life-hacking approach. Frankly, this version of the question speaks to me more deeply than I like to admit, as there is nothing like the feeling that comes at the beginning of one's latest self-improvement campaign. For can-do, bootstrapping, nose-to-the-grindstone academics, such strategies can be a heady source of hope and direction. In addition to making us feel good, these time-management tools *do* good. They provide effective strategies for making good use of our time. But a sole reliance on life hacking can sometimes capitulate to the injustice of academic working conditions. For, in using these strategies, we find both relief from our circumstances and a reproduction of them. On the one hand, time management strategies may make us more efficient, thereby proving we actually *could* get more done in the time we have available, if only we would try. On the other hand, our use of these strategies implies that the demand to squeeze more tasks into the same amount of time is legitimate. It assumes that doing so is beneficial, both for the human and the writing—even though models of the creative process show that more work doesn't necessarily equal better work. And it ignores how excessive work demands create or exacerbate damage to our families, relationships, mental well-being, and bodies.

Because, as a writing coach, I advocate the use of these techniques, it's also my responsibility to admit their limits. It's especially my responsibility to do so since independent writing coaches are as much a part of the problem as we are a condemnation of and partial solution to it. The need for our support has sprung up in the absence of adequate university support for writing (Nzinga, 2020). And what we offer should be the *base level of university support provided to every scholar,* regardless of their seniority or contract status. By providing our services to scholars who can afford them, we inevitably reinforce the institutional and social hierarchies that give scholars unequal access to the knowledge and support that influence professional advancement. Our existence also makes it easier for universities to abdicate their responsibilities to faculty and graduate students.

I'd therefore like to use this final chapter to ask, not the small life-hacking question, but the larger, life-enhancing question. To explore how you can step outside the demand for machine-like productivity and create the conditions needed to follow your own writing process. This book has argued that we get stuck when we misinterpret writing difficulties as personal failures and subsequently relinquish our writing process. Yet it also suggests a strategy for getting unstuck that might feel like an even bigger risk. It asks you to explore a writing process that will take time to develop. It suggests you practice *making mistakes* with that process. Given all I've said about how the structure of academic work makes risk-taking difficult, how can you create the private space in your mind—the time, the quiet, the solitude and fortitude—that will allow you to develop and trust your own writing process?

The Promise and Perils of Slow Scholarship

I am not the first scholar to ask this question. The slow scholarship literature suggest that not only is it *possible* to write without capitulating to demands for overwork, but that in fact, it's *required* if you want to excel as a scholar. Mountz et al., for example, urge scholars to push back against the "wildly outsized expectations of productivity," and instead make time to think and write, as well as to "reach for the minimum" (Mountz et al., 2015, pp. 1252–1253). *The Slow Professor* authors Berg and Seeber suggest another way to respond to unreasonable work demands: stop focusing on the *efficient* use of time and instead focus on our *enhanced experience* of time (2016). Instead of trying to get more done during our writing sessions, we should instead work to immerse ourselves more fully in our writing sessions, thereby experiencing more enjoyment while simultaneously completing more work. In doing so, they draw on research about flow, which illustrates that when we are fully immersed in our experiences, we not only enjoy them more, but also produce higher-quality work.

This strategy of focusing on experience over efficiency is especially instructive, because it highlights the fact that our individual choices about how to work as writers are also a form of political stance taking. In other words, when you make time to develop your writing process, you are not just writing. You are also choosing, at that moment, to ignore the institutional and professional pressures to overwork and overproduce. You're deciding to move with more care and deliberation in your writing, despite the possible negative consequences that come with prioritizing the quality of your experience over the pace of your production (Ahmed, 2014). In other words, slowing down not only provides the much-needed rest and relief that enhances the quality of scholarship, but in a system dependent on the degradation and misuse of the body, the choice to slow down and follow your process is also a choice to reject the validity of the narratives that force us to prioritize speed over quality and well-being (even though ultimately, we must contend with them).

Despite many scholars' desire to do just that, two barriers can challenge their ability to carve out the space for an enhanced experience of time. The first is that adopting the most commonly suggested strategies of slow scholarship can often feel impossible. When graduation, reputation, tenure-track jobs, and promotion hang in the balance, junior scholars feel too vulnerable to take the chance of not overextending themselves. The second pattern I've observed is that, even when a scholar *is* willing to try a slow scholarship approach to their writing, they are immediately faced with a second dilemma—one they rarely see, but that has become more apparent to me over my last decade of coaching. And that is, a slow scholarship approach often cannot be consistently enacted without a concomitant shift in one's sense of entitlement.

By entitlement, I do not mean the sense that one is owed special favors or treatment. By entitlement, I mean the belief that one has a right to something. Put more plainly, many scholars feel they do not have the right to write. They feel pressure to produce. To publish. To finish. To get projects into the pipeline. But they do not necessarily feel they have the right to do the long, slow, one-step-forward, two-steps-back writing required to make a manuscript ready for Submission.

The scholars I work with do not use these words. They would not put it this way. What they say is that it's too hard to get to the writing when their students need so much from them. They say how hard it is to take time away from their kids. They say their graduate students need feedback or a letter of recommendation—immediately. They say they have to check their email at the beginning of the day, because their coauthors might think they're not working if they don't respond quickly enough to messages. They say they can't close the door to their office because, as department chair, they have to be available in case their faculty, coauthors, assistant, or RA needs something from them. In a thousand different ways, they say that the work of writing cannot come before any of the other work that is being asked of them. Even when deprioritizing their writing hurts them professionally and robs them of the pleasure of engaging in their project.

I see this lack of entitlement with many of the scholars I work with. And I see a specific version of it among people of color and those who come from working-class families or communities with a history of colonialism, hardship, disinvestment, and annihilation. For these scholars, the focus on self required to put one's writing first—thinking of your needs; being unavailable; deliberately incorporating rest into your day; and doing all this even when it inconveniences or annoys others—this behavior stinks of a self-indulgence they cannot wrap their minds around. These activities seem like the pillows of privilege instead of the basic foundations of a writer's life. Not because the scholar is a doormat; but because their lives, their scholarship, their politics—indeed their own personal success, is rooted in communities that have survived and excelled precisely because of their collective orientation.[2]

And yet, over the last ten years, I've watched scholars move from being stuck and scared to trusting their process. I've watched them go from checking email on their phone immediately after their alarm goes off to not bothering to look at it until long past noon. I've watched them move from being too terrified to open their manuscript to writing regularly, even in the worst of circumstances. These changes are not merely the result of a strategic alignment of time with values. Instead, they tend to reflect an *internal* shift, an insistence that they have the right, not just to write, but also to prioritize their well-being over reactive attempts to please—even though that right is a form of privilege. Until writers develop this sense of entitlement, the other behavioral shifts we make are often on shaky ground. How then, can you develop the willingness to take the risks *Becoming* asks you to take? How do you strengthen the sense of entitlement needed to take them? One change that helps immensely is to develop an oppositional writer's consciousness.

Writer's Oppositional Consciousness

An oppositional consciousness is an awareness that the conditions one faces are unjust and a commitment to changing those conditions. In discussing writers' oppositional consciousness I'm adapting a framework used by social movement scholars to understand what leads people to take risks and make sacrifices for the welfare of the group (Mansbridge & Morris, 2001). Scholarship on oppositional consciousness has examined its prevalence for many marginalized groups including African Americans, women, immigrants, and people with disabilities. So, it might seem a stretch to borrow from a social movement concept when examining the position of academic writers—people who have attained or are in the process of attaining some of the most protected jobs available and who are not using writing to liberate other academics from a system of domination. Yet there are two aspects of academic life that make this a useful framework for understanding how to develop an "entitled" approach to writing. The first is that, as social movement scholars point out, oppositional consciousness is essentially a resource that helps individuals understand their circumstances, so that actions that previously seemed too risky feel doable and possible. At root, an oppositional consciousness is something that academic writers can draw on to become more willing to bear the risks of experimenting with our process; prioritizing our writing; or even choosing to put our health and wellbeing ahead of our department's expectations for tenure.

Another condition that makes the idea of oppositional consciousness useful for thinking through an academic writer's situation is that, unlike those who write largely in response to a creative calling, university scholars write in response to job demands that are themselves a significant source of their difficulties with writing. Regardless of where you teach, the demand to publish, teach, serve, and lead more, all come from the same institution. Therefore, it makes sense for writers to work to understand their writing life in relationship to the institution within which they work. Holding an oppositional consciousness, therefore, can help us understand our relationship to the evaluation system and social hierarchies that make writing even harder than it already is.

It's important to note that a writer's oppositional consciousness is not fundamentally an opposition to individuals who hold administrative positions. I am not suggesting that all administrators are your enemies. What I'm suggesting is that scholars with a strong oppositional consciousness are clear that the interests of the university and their interests as individuals do not necessarily overlap. They understand that they are attempting to write in a context that may actually make writing *more* rather than less difficult. And as a result, they are better able to see how their writing lives are influenced by job scarcity, social hierarchies, and uneven demands for overwork.

Social movement scholars define oppositional consciousness as existing when group members "claim their previously subordinate identity as a positive identification, identify injustices done to their group, demand changes in the polity, economy, or society to rectify injustices, and see other members of their group as sharing an interest in rectifying those injustices" (Mansbridge & Morris, 2001, p. 1). I suggest that a writer's consciousness includes four similar elements: claiming a writer's identity, identifying unfairness, refusing to comply, and seeing shared struggle.

Claiming a Writer's Identity

Scholars with an oppositional writers' consciousness see themselves as writers. That is, they see writing as a distinct part of their work, understanding and labeling themselves as scholars, researchers, *and* writers. When scholars explicitly *claim* a writer's identity, it's not necessarily the first time they're *holding* a writing identity. As Kate Evans points out, "In some ways, whenever we write, we take on an 'identity' as a writer. We may identify ourselves as a non-writer, a good writer, a bad writer, a struggling writer. These notions of us as a writer will be developed by past experience and feedback" (Evans, 2013, p. 46). What's significant about *this* writing identity is that it is a deliberate statement of who they understand themselves to be, not a judgment about their worth as writers.

One particularly strong form of writing identity I have seen, is scholars who have a commitment to their writing that lies beyond the tenure-track. In other words, while these scholars pursue and value the benefits of promotion and tenure, those rewards are not the only ones they pursue. They understand academia as their job, not their work. So, their faculty position is the container within which they do their writing. But it is the writing that matters most. Poets who are also literature scholars. Sociologists in "article departments" who prioritize writing field-defining books. Public health scientists who prioritize public advocacy over university promotion. It's not that these scholars feel free to dismiss the requirements for tenure. It's that they *understand* their work—and therefore their writing—as separate from the institutional reward system.

Identifying Unfairness

The second element of an oppositional writer's consciousness is the ability to identify unfairness in the demands their departments and institutions place on them. Theories of the corporatized university and the academic as neoliberal subject are certainly helpful in giving scholars a general sense of the situation facing the profession. But in order for scholars to respond differently, they must be able to actually *see* when their situation constitutes an instance of unfairness, excessive demand, or social inequality. An example would be an assistant professor who notes the lack of mentors she can go to for advice, and the limited writing time she has available each day. And instead of assuming that she is "doing something wrong," she sees those conditions as related to the lack of affordable childcare, or the fact that the university's childcare program closes before the late afternoon receptions and talks that are the primary relationship-building moments in her department. In short, she can *contextualize* rather than *personalize* the challenges she encounters. Being able to identify these conditions and their relationship to her writing makes it easier for her to seek solutions that free up time rather than blaming herself for the conditions in the first place.

Refusing to Comply

Academics with a strong writer's consciousness also insist on changes to rectify the situation. The primary demand I have observed among scholars with a writer's consciousness is that their time is their own. That their professional obligations to others do not automatically come first or trump their own priorities and certainly do not come before their health or well-being. Instead of assuming they need to be constantly available to others because other people are having a problem, they decide that their time belongs to them and that they have the right to do with it what they choose. These refusals do not look especially heroic. In fact, they're quite commonplace for men who have been socialized to see their time as valuable. Refusals take place when faculty members mark themselves as unavailable for service meetings because they take place during their writing time; when they close their office doors and do not respond when someone knocks. These are small, everyday acts through which they set and hold boundaries against the incursions on their time. But they are enormously powerful, as they reflect scholar's unwillingness to sacrifice their writing time for the competing demands that can easily swallow that time.

Seeing Shared Struggle

The final element of a writer's consciousness is that scholars see themselves as sharing similar struggles with other academic writers. They come to see that not every writer has the exact same problem. And that even when they have similar problems, they don't experience or respond to them in the same way. In short, they recognize the lie behind their sense that they are an imposter. And they understand that even those who have mastered certain aspects of writing have done so after long, hard work to overcome their barriers.

Each of these dimensions of an oppositional writer's consciousness exists on a continuum.[3] It's entirely possible, for example, that the scholar who refuses the meeting during her writing time will also binge-write to meet a journal deadline. As is the case with any transformation, the change comes in halting, uneven steps. Yet, the elements of an oppositional consciousness are an internal resource that we can call on to carve out time and space and follow our process, even when that process is slow, the outcomes uncertain, and we're working under a deadline. In short, a writer's consciousness helps you do the slow, difficult, risky work of uncovering and following your writing process.

In addition, scholars vary in the degree to which they understand oppositional consciousness as a political stance. For some, an oppositional writer's consciousness is an approach they take to secure tenure and promotion. This impulse makes sense, given the conditions described in Chapter 2. The danger in this orientation is that developing this orientation becomes just one more way those scholars end up taking individual responsibility for unfair circumstances created by the university. In this sense, it's an instance of what Ahmed (citing Lourde) describes as self-care functioning as "a technique of governance: the duty to care for one's self often written as a duty to care for one's own happiness, flourishing, wellbeing" (Ahmed, 2014).

Other scholars adopt an oppositional writer's consciousness as a deliberate way to gain legitimacy in a system they want to change. They do so in the same way that feminists have developed citational, networking, and review practices. What distinguishes their activities "is a sense of organization, commitment, and solidarity . . . a shared notion that this was done as part of a cohesive political action" (Burton, 2018, p. 118). When Mountz et al. call on scholars to take more time, for example, they specify that senior scholars should be the ones to do this, so they can open up a conversation on behalf of junior scholars that legitimizes the decision to emphasize quality over quantity (2015).

A third way that scholars adopt an oppositional writer's consciousness is with the explicit desire to *resist or refuse* the logic and pressure of work intensification. Again, these show up as fairly mundane, but still significant decisions about how to spend one's time (as well as how to *think and feel* about that expenditure of time). Moving back submission deadlines—without shame—in response to immune system flare-ups; taking time to thoroughly read fewer texts, instead of creating an exhaustive literature review. Persistently performing and documenting requests for COVID extensions on a tenure clock, based on the research showing its disproportionate impact on women. The point is not that these actions lead to system change. Nor am I suggesting that scholars can engage in these behaviors without consequence. The point is that, if you choose to, you can use these moments in your writing practice to consciously act against the pressures to overwork—in ways that actually prioritize your writing practice.

These last two ways of adopting an oppositional writer's consciousness might feel more familiar and attainable for scholars who are already embedded in other justice communities. If your scholarship, service, or political work are concerned with dismantling patterns of dominance, you likely have a wide range of supportive relationships that you can use as a model for oppositional consciousness. While scholars who lack mentors and advocates in the tenure process; who are the "only" in their department; or whose vision of strong scholarship radically differs from that of their department may find it makes most sense to use a writer's consciousness to establish their legitimacy. Whatever your relationship to your institution, oppositional writer's consciousness offers a framework for shifting your perspective in ways that help you move away from the sense that we are powerless before the demands of our institutions.

Making Space With Social Writing

It's certainly possible to develop an oppositional writer's consciousness on your own. But an easier, more pleasurable, and more effective way to do so is to become a Social Writer. Social writing happens when people come together in a protected space to write—and reflect on writing—in a structured way.[4] For example, writing in a café together, "Skype Writing" (writing on a Zoom call), attending a writing retreat, or even "texting-in" (checking in by text) throughout a writing session with your co-writer. In each case, regardless of the platform used or length of communication, you can create the safety and structure you need to engage in two key activities: the first is companionship—writing alongside other scholars. The second is reflection—sharing your thoughts about the writing experience.

We already know that social writing can boost writers' productivity and positive experience of writing.[5] What receives less attention is how social writing strengthens our ability to develop a writer's consciousness. Social movement literature shows that people develop an oppositional consciousness when they talk with those who already hold this interpretive lens; when they engage in collective action together; and when they see for themselves the positive effects of their collective labor. Similarly, social writing can help scholars develop an oppositional consciousness by creating the time, relationships, and interactions that support it.

The first way social writing does this is through the deceptively simple act of creating time and space to write. Because it involves making a commitment, showing up, and doing the actual work together, social writing is a powerful way to develop your writing identity, the first component of writer's consciousness. This is true even when you have very small amounts of writing time available: I frequently encourage writers returning home from retreats to aim for "Tiny Bite Writing." These are small snippets of five, fifteen, perhaps twenty minutes of writing—whatever can genuinely be squeezed into the day, even if everything goes wrong. Most detest the idea—yet many are amazed to find several weeks later that their Tiny Bite Writing practice regular and reliable, and they *feel* more like a writer (even as they hold anxiety about meeting deadlines). This identity transformation happens in part because our professional identities are shaped by what we do—the small, repeated acts we engage in. But these identities are also influenced by our professional circles: scholars write regularly with a group of writers—and are therefore writers themselves. This is where regular social writing (for example, regular co-writing sessions) shines: It is the *repeated enactment* of even short bursts of writing that help scholars cultivate a writing identity.

A second way social writing helps develop a writer's consciousness is by helping us see unfairness. This is where the reflective process between writing partners is essential, because it challenges the belief that the struggles with writing are particular to you. What the literature shows, and what I have observed over and over at retreats, is that asking other scholars about their process and *hearing* them reflect on their struggles has a transformative effect on writers. In a way that cannot be produced merely through verbal reassurance, listening to others recount writing challenges and struggles you have experienced powerfully convinces scholars that they are not the problem. Have you ever been in that situation where you can easily identify how external conditions hamper your colleagues—but are less able to see their effect on you? Social writing gives you the benefit of other scholars who are able to analyze your position and point out the ways that your writing challenges are context-driven, not personal. This is especially the case when the scholar sharing their experience is held in high esteem, either because of their position or their reputation. And this pattern of *seeing* what really gets in the way of writing is often the key to scholar's ability to stop personalizing their writing struggles as individual failures and instead contextualize them as artifacts of writing and their writing environment.

A third way that social writing helps develop a writer's consciousness is by helping us see each other's shared struggle. Watching others encounter, wrestle with, and overcome their own writing struggles helps scholars develop confidence in their ability to do the same (MacLeod et al., 2011; Zimmerman & Kitsantas, 2002). But it provides an embodied experience that is far more convincing than just reading or being told that "everyone struggles with writing." Watching others struggle then succeed, then having your own experience of struggling-then-succeeding is what Zumbrunn (2021) calls a "mastery experience,"—your own instance of encountering and overcoming a problem that builds confidence and counters the narrative that you're "Just not cut out for this work." In other words, social writing takes the hope provided by this book, accepts the doubt that scholars feel, then converts it into a lived experience you can feel, remember, and draw upon for years to come.

A final way that social writing helps scholars cultivate a writing consciousness is by providing opportunities to refuse demands on their time and instead prioritize process over product. Social writing provides space and structure for scholars to explore their writing process in pursuit of Flow and Forward Writing instead. In short, it helps scholars enact Berg and Seeber's "enhanced experience" (2016) of writing time, especially when it's structured by a facilitator. Once scholars have learned a workable structure, they can transfer it to their regular writing sessions (MacLeod, 2011; Murray, 2014). At our retreats, for example, I identify the five main Pivot Points of a writing session—the most challenging and potentially derailing moments of a session—and provide tools that participants can use to overcome those challenges. Once scholars learn to "see" their writing session through the lens of that structure, they can more easily identify what's happening when a problem arises; and they have strategies at their fingertips for overcoming those challenges. In other words, social writing provides the perfect container in which to use the "Practice First" strategy discussed in Chapter 5: exploring, experimenting with, and enhancing your writing process.

In short, when we write with others, we don't just get our writing done. We build a community of practice whose members help each other shift their perspectives about writing. So that instead of seeing writing difficulties as the result of individual weakness, you may more clearly understand the institutional conditions and inherent challenges that keep you from being the writer you want to be. Instead of feeling at the mercy of all the demands on your time, you feel more comfortable putting your writing first. Instead of dismissing your writing process because it feels incomplete or quirky or circuitous, you can accept the time it takes to develop and express complex ideas—and then work through the discomfort that comes with doing so. You might even, as Anne Tyler did when she was told about her Pulitzer Prize, enjoy the delicious thrill of external recognition, while staying sweetly attuned to the urgency of your own writing experience.

Scholars can't rely on universities to provide this kind of community. University administrators, boards of trustees—even the deans and department heads whom we like and respect, and who are genuinely committed to supporting our career—all share an interest in increasing your output. They do not share an interest in helping you build a sustainable writing life. And while coaches can provide an entree into this approach to writing, we should be a temporary support, one that takes scholars to the point where we are no longer needed. Social Writing with friends and colleagues can be a strong, supportive counterweight to the professional socialization and reward processes that push scholars to place productivity above all. It allows scholars to build new connections, new identities, and new definitions of success that support not just your productivity, but your unique process. I know that suggesting Social Writing as a way to make space for the writing life you want puts yet another burden on already overburdened scholars. However, what I've found is that when scholars do not actively work to construct our *own* ideal writing identity, we find ourselves at the mercy of the passive construction of identity that happens when we enter the profession.

Writing is hard, there are no two ways about it. If you ask some of the scholars who've been through the Metaphor workshop, they'll tell you that for them, writing is a roller coaster. It's a shepherd herding sheep. It's being dropped off in a strange place with no map (or using multiple maps that are all written in different languages). It's finding your way through a maze. It's a Marie Kondo decluttering session. It's planning a dinner party. It's weeding a beautiful garden. It's housetraining your puppy. It's all those things and it's none of those, depending on who you are. Because what writing is most of all, is yours. No one else gets to tell you what it should look like, or how you should bring it into the world. You get to decide who you are as a writer and the place that writing will have in your life. Your writing belongs entirely to you. Watch what happens when you claim it.

Notes

1. www.baltimoresun.com/entertainment/bs-fe-Anne-Tyler-interview-20220320-jxsp43hw55fonajy63ua53wqau-story.html

2. Certainly scholars can change their approach to writing without this sense of entitlement. We are motivated by fear, aspiration, ambition, duty, joy, and a host of other feelings. My point is that underneath it all, scholars need to feel that taking time away from other activities is legitimate, regardless of whether they are stuck in their writing or not.

3. As is the case with social movement actors (Mansbridge & Morris, 2001, p. 238).

4. See Murray (2014) as well as Aitchison and Guerin, who use a slightly broader definition of what they call "writing groups," "an umbrella generic term to refer to situations where more than two people come together to work on their writing in a sustained way, over repeated gatherings, for doing, discussing or sharing their writing for agreed purposes" (2014, p. 7).

5. Among their many benefits is their capacity to reduce anxiety (MacLeod et al., 2011) increase productivity (Murray & Newton, 2009), boost motivation (Moore, 2003), build a sense of community—and provide a basis for continued productivity after returning to daily life (Murray, 2014).

• References •

Adams, S. (2013, January 3). *The least stressful jobs of 2013*. Forbes. Retrieved April 4, 2022, from https://www.forbes.com/sites/susanadams/2013/01/03/the-least-stressful-jobs-of-2013/

Ahmed, S. (2014, August 25). *Selfcare as Warfare*. feministkilljoys. Retrieved April 15, 2022, from https://feministkilljoys.com/2014/08/25/selfcare-as-warfare/

Ahmed, S. J. (2019). An analysis of writer's block: Causes, characteristics, solutions. *UNF Graduate Theses and Dissertations, 903*. Retrieved from https://digitalcommons.unf.edu/etd/903.

Aitchison, C., & Guerin, C. (2014). *Writing Groups for Doctoral Education and Beyond: Innovations in Practice and Theory*. Routledge.

Amabile, T. M., & Kramer, S. J. (2011). *The Progress Principle: Using Small Wins to Ignite Joy, Engagement, and Creativity at Work*. Harvard Business Review Press.

An Army of Temps: AFT 2020 Adjunct Faculty Quality of Work/Life Report. American Federation of Teachers. (2020). Retrieved April 11, 2022, from https://www.aft.org/sites/default/files/adjuncts_qualityworklife2020.pdf

Anderson, T., Saunders, G., & Alexander, I. (2021). Alternative dissertation formats in education-based doctorates. *Higher Education Research & Development*, 1–20. https://doi.org/10.1080/07294360.2020.1867513

Antoniou, M., & Moriarty, J. (2008). What can academic writers learn from creative writers?: Developing guidance and support for lecturers in higher education. *Teaching in Higher Education, 13*(2), 157–167. https://doi.org/10.1080/13562510801923229

Anzaldúa, G. (2003). In G. A. Olson & L. Worsham (Eds.), *Critical Intellectuals on Writing* (pp. 15–29). State University of New York Press.

Arora, T. (2010). Writing as a process: An interview with Mike Rose. *InterActions: UCLA Journal of Education and Information Studies, 6*(2). https://doi.org/10.5070/d462000680

Atwood, M. (2002). *Negotiating with the Dead: A Writer on Writing*. Cambridge University Press.

Badley, G. (2009). Academic writing as shaping and re-shaping. *Teaching in Higher Education, 14*(2), 209–219. https://doi.org/10.1080/13562510902757294

Bane, R. (2012). *Around the Writer's Block: Using Brain Science to Solve Writer's Resistance*. Tarcher Perigee.

Barakat, M., & Rodríguez, M. A. (2021). *Immigrant Faculty in the Academy: Narratives of Identity, Resilience, and Action*. Routledge.

Barreca, G. (2011, May 23). Bribes and guilt as tools for writing. *The Chronicle of Higher Education*. Retrieved April 14, 2022, from https://www.chronicle.com/blogs/brainstorm/bribes-and-guilt-as-tools-for-writing

Bartholomae, D. (1985). Inventing the University. In M. Rose (Ed.), *When a Writer Can't Write* (pp. 134–165). The Guilford Press.

Becker, H. S. (1986). *Writing for Social Scientists: How to Start and Finish Your Thesis, Book, or Article*. University of Chicago Press.

Being diagnosed with adult ADHD as a professor. Spatial Determinants of Health Lab. (2019, April 22). Retrieved April 12, 2022, from https://carleton.ca/determinants/?p=463

Belcher, W. L. (2009). *Writing Your Journal Article in Twelve Weeks: A Guide to Academic Publishing Success*. SAGE Publications.

Berg, M., & Seeber, B. K. (2016). *The Slow Professor: Challenging the Culture of Speed in the Academy*. Toronto University Press.

Boice, R. (1990). Faculty resistance to writing-intensive courses. *Teaching of Psychology, 17*(1), 13–17. https://doi.org/10.1207/s15328023top1701_3

Boice, R. (1994). *How Writers Journey from Comfort to Fluency: A Psychological Adventure*. Praeger.

Boice, R., & Jones, F. (1984). Why Academicians Don't Write. *The Journal of Higher Education, 55*(5), 567–582. https://doi.org/https://doi.org/10.2307/1981822

Bolton, G. (2014). *Reflective Practice: Writing and Professional Development* (4th ed.). SAGE Publications.

Bolton, G., & Rowland, S. (2014). *Inspirational Writing for Academic Publication*. SAGE Publications.

Boyd, M. (2012). How we write: Understanding scholarly writing through metaphor. *PS: Political Science & Politics, 45*(4), 736–741. https://doi.org/10.1017/s1049096512000832

Bravata, D. M., Watts, S. A., Keefer, A. L., Madhusudhan, D. K., Taylor, K. T., Clark, D. M., Nelson, R. S., Cokley, K. O., & Hagg, H. K. (2020). Prevalence, predictors, and treatment of impostor syndrome: A systematic review. *Journal of General Internal Medicine, 35*(4), 1252–1275. https://doi.org/10.1007/s11606-019-05364-1

Burton, S. (2018). Writing yourself in? The price of playing the (feminist) game in the neoliberal university. *Feeling Academic in the Neoliberal University*, 115–136. https://doi.org/10.1007/978-3-319-64224-6_6

Carnell, E., MacDonald, J., McCallum, B., & Scott, M. (2008). *Passion and Politics: Academics Reflect on Writing for Publication*. University of London Institute of Education Press.

Ciampa, K., & Wolfe, Z. (2019). Preparing for dissertation writing: Doctoral education students' perceptions. *Studies in Graduate and Postdoctoral Education, 10*(2), 86–108. https://doi.org/10.1108/sgpe-03-2019-0039

Clance, P. R., & Imes, S. A. (1978). The imposter phenomenon in high achieving women: Dynamics and therapeutic intervention. *Psychotherapy: Theory, Research & Practice, 15*(3), 241–247. https://doi.org/10.1037/h0086006

Csikszentmihalyi, M. (1990). *Flow: The Psychology of Optimal Experience.* Harper and Row.

Data Snapshot: Contingent Faculty in US higher Ed. American Association of University Professors. (2018). Retrieved April 11, 2022, from https://www.aaup.org/sites/default/files/10112018%20Data%20Snapshot%20Tenure.pdf?elqTrackId=821261a0 2dd04de7956245f69731a3ac&elq=dd050fa6e7c4464bb372a1ea43e4fe65&elqaid=2 0941&elqat=1&elqCampaignId=9917

Davis, J. (2015). *Two Awesome Hours: Science-based Strategies to Harness Your Best Time and Get Your Most Important Work Done.* HarperOne.

de Novais, J. (2018). Doctor of vulnerability and resilience. In S. A. Shelton, J. E. Flynn, & T. J. Grosland (Eds.), *Feminism and intersectionality in academia: Women's narratives and experiences in higher education* (pp. 167–178). Palgrave Macmillan.

Dennett, D. C. (2014). *Intuition Pumps and Other Tools for Thinking.* Penguin Books.

Diers-Lawson, A. (2013, January 4). *The Least Stressful Job for 2013? A Real Look at Being a Professor in the US.* Facts & Other Fairy Tales. Retrieved April 4, 2022, from https://factsandotherfairytales.wordpress.com/2013/01/04/the-least-stressful-job-for-2013-a-real-look-at-being-a-professor-in-the-us/

Dillard, A. (1989). *The Writing Life.* HarperCollins.

Dunlap, L. (2007). *Undoing the Silence: Six Tools for Social Change Writing.* New Village Press.

Eells, W. C. (1962). The origin and early history of sabbatical leave. *AAUP Bulletin, 48*(3), 253–256. https://doi.org/10.2307/40222893

El-Alayli, A., Hansen-Brown, A. A., & Ceynar, M. (2018). Dancing backwards in high heels: Female professors experience more work demands and special favor requests, particularly from academically entitled students. *Sex Roles, 79*(3–4), 136–150. https://doi.org/10.1007/s11199-017-0872-6

Emerson, R. M., Fretz, R. I., & Shaw, L. L. (1995). *Writing Ethnographic Fieldnotes.* The University of Chicago Press.

Eraut, M. (2000). Non-formal learning, implicit learning and tacit knowledge in professional work. In F. Coffield (Ed.), *The Necessity of Informal Learning* (pp. 12–31). Policy Press.

Evans, K. (2013). *Pathways Through Writing Blocks in the Academic Environment.* Sense Publishers.

Feenstra, S., Begeny, C. T., Ryan, M. K., Rink, F. A., Stoker, J. I., & Jordan, J. (2020). Contextualizing the impostor "syndrome." *Frontiers in Psychology, 11.* https://doi.org/10.3389/fpsyg.2020.575024

Fergie, G., Beeke, S., McKenna, C., & Creme, P. (2011). "It's a lonely walk": Supporting postgraduate researchers through writing. *International Journal of Teaching and Learning in Higher Education, 23*(2), 236–245.

Ferrales, G., & Fine, G. A. (2005). Sociology as a vocation: Reputations and group cultures in graduate school. *The American Sociologist, 36*(2), 57–75. https://doi.org/10.1007/s12108-005-1005-1

Fitzgerald, C. M. (2015). Downtime. In G. C. Semenza & G. A. Sullivan (Eds.), *How to Build a Life in the Humanities: Meditations on the Academic Work-Life Balance* (pp. 101–108). Palgrave Macmillan.

Flaherty, C. (2014, April 9). *So much to do, so little time.* Inside Higher Ed. Retrieved April 4, 2022, from https://www.insidehighered.com/news/2014/04/09/research-shows-professors-work-long-hours-and-spend-much-day-meetings

Flaherty, C. (2021, February 17). What's really going on with respect to bias and teaching evals? Retrieved April 11, 2022, from https://www.insidehighered.com/news/2021/02/17/whats-really-going-respect-bias-and-teaching-evals

Flores Niemann, Y. (2012). The making of a token: A case study of stereotype threat, stigma, racism, and tokenism in academe. In G. y Muhs Gutiérrez, Y. Flores Niemann, C. G. González, & A. P. Harris (Eds.), *Presumed Incompetent: The Intersections of Race and Class for Women in Academia* (pp. 336–355). Utah State University Press.

Flower, L. S., & Hayes, J. R. (2016). The dynamics of composing: Making plans and juggling constraints. In E. R. Steinberg & L. W. Gregg (Eds.), *Cognitive Processes in Writing* (pp. 31–50). Routledge.

Forester, J. (1984). (Circulated unpublished until included in Silvia et al. 2014). Learning the Craft of Academic Writing: Notes on Writing In and After Graduate School.

Gërxhani, K., Kulic, N., & Liechti, F. (2021). Double standards? Co-authorship and gender bias in early stage academic hiring. *LIVES Working Papers, 86,* 1–32. https://doi.org/10.12682/lives.2296-1658.2020.86

Goodson, P. (2013). *Becoming an Academic Writer: 50 Exercises for Paced, Productive, and Powerful Writing.* SAGE Publications.

Gray, T. (2005). *Publish & Flourish: Become a Prolific Scholar.* Teaching Academy New Mexico State University.

Hardman, J. (2021). From South America to South Florida: Risks and rewards for senior international students. In M. Barakat and M. Rodríguez (Eds.), *Immigrant Faculty in the Academy: Narratives of Identity, Resilience, and Action.* Routledge.

Hayot, E. (2014). *The Elements of Academic Style: Writing for the Humanities*. Columbia University Press.

Hitz, Z. (2020). *Lost in Thought: The Hidden Pleasures of an Intellectual Life*. Princeton University Press.

Hjortshoj, K. (2001). *Understanding Writing Blocks*. Oxford University Press.

Houston, N. M. (2015). Imposter phenomenon. In G. C. Semenza & G. A. Sullivan (Eds.), *How to Build a Life in the Humanities: Meditations on the Academic Work-Life Balance* (pp. 73–81). Palgrave Macmillan.

Hyland, K. (2008). Genre and academic writing in the disciplines. *Language Teaching, 41*(4), 543–562. https://doi.org/10.1017/s0261444808005235

Ibarra, H. (2004). *Working Identity: Unconventional Strategies for Reinventing Your Career*. Harvard Business School Press.

Janesick, V. J. (2011). *"Stretching" Exercises for Qualitative Researchers*. SAGE Publications.

Jensen, J. (2017). *Write No Matter What: Advice for Academics*. The University of Chicago Press.

Kamler, B., & Thomson, P. (2008). The failure of dissertation advice books: Toward alternative pedagogies for doctoral writing. *Educational Researcher, 37*(8), 507–514. https://doi.org/10.3102/0013189x08327390

Kamler, B., & Thomson, P. (2014). *Helping Doctoral Students Write: Pedagogies for Supervision*. Routledge.

Kellogg, R. T. (1986). Writing method and productivity of science and engineering Faculty. *Research in Higher Education, 25*(2), 147–163. https://doi.org/10.1007/bf00991488

Kounios, J., & Beeman, M. (2015). *The Eureka Factor: Creative Insights and the Brain*. Cornerstone Digital.

Langin, K. (2019, March 12). *In a first, U.S. private sector employs nearly as many Ph.D.s as schools do*. Science. Retrieved April 11, 2022, from https://www.science.org/content/article/first-us-private-sector-employs-nearly-many-phds-schools-do

Larson, R. C., Ghaffarzadegan, N., & Xue, Y. (2013). Too many PhD graduates or too few academic job openings: The basic reproductive number R0 in Academia. *Systems Research and Behavioral Science, 31*(6), 745–750. https://doi.org/10.1002/sres.2210

Lindsey, P., & Crusan, D. (2011). How faculty attitudes and expectations toward student nationality affect writing assessment. *Across the Disciplines, 8*(4), 1–19. https://doi.org/10.37514/atd-j.2011.8.4.23

MacLeod, I., Steckley, L., & Murray, R. (2011). Time is not enough: Promoting strategic engagement with writing for publication. *Studies in Higher Education, 37*(6), 641–654. https://doi.org/10.1080/03075079.2010.527934

Malamud Smith, J. (2012). *An Absorbing Errand: How Artists and Craftsmen Make Their Way to Mastery.* Counterpoint.

Mansbridge, J. J., & Morris, A. D. (2001). *Oppositional Consciousness: The Subjective Roots of Social Protest.* University of Chicago Press.

Matthew, C. T., & Sternberg, R. J. (2009). Developing experience-based (tacit) knowledge through reflection. *Learning and Individual Differences, 19*(4), 530–540. https://doi.org/10.1016/j.lindif.2009.07.001

Matthew, P. A. (2016). *Written/Unwritten: Diversity and the hidden truths of tenure.* University of North Carolina Press.

McKenna, L. (2018, February 7). How hard do professors actually work? *The Atlantic.* Retrieved April 5, 2022, from https://www.theatlantic.com/education/archive/2018/02/how-hard-do-professors-actually-work/552698/

Mohr, T. (2014). *Playing Big: Find Your Voice, Your Vision and Make Things Happen.* Hutchinson.

Moore, S. (2003). Writers' retreats for academics: Exploring and increasing the motivation to write. *Journal of Further and Higher Education, 27*(3), 333–342. https://doi.org/10.1080/0309877032000098734

Morgan, J. (2012, August 2). *How do academics spend their time? Filling out forms about how they spend their time.* The World University Rankings. Retrieved from https://www.timeshighereducation.com/news/how-do-academics-spend-their-time-filling-out-forms-about-how-they-spend-their-time-/420752.article

Mountz, A., Bonds, A., Mansfield, B., Loyd, J., Hyndman, J., Walton-Roberts, M., Basu, R., Whitson, R., Hawkins, R., Hamilton, T., & Curran, W. (2015). For slow scholarship: A feminist politics of resistance through collective action in the neoliberal university. *ACME: An International Journal for Critical Geographies, 14,* 1235–1259.

Muradoglu, M., Horne, Z., Hammond, M. D., Leslie, S.-J., & Cimpian, A. (2021). Women—particularly underrepresented minority women—and early-career academics feel like impostors in fields that value brilliance. *Journal of Educational Psychology.* https://doi.org/10.1037/edu0000669

Murray, D. M. (1978). Write before writing. *College Composition and Communication, 29*(4), 375–381. https://doi.org/https://doi.org/10.2307/357024

Murray, D. M. (1992). *Read to Write: A Writing Process Reader.* Holt, Rinehart, and Winston.

Murray, R. (2014). *Writing in Social Spaces: A Social Processes Approach to Academic Writing.* Routledge.

Murray, R., & Newton, M. (2009). Writing retreat as structured intervention: Margin or mainstream? *Higher Education Research & Development, 28*(5), 541–553. https://doi.org/10.1080/07294360903154126

Nagoski, E., & Nagoski, A. (2020). *Burnout: The Secret to Unlocking the Stress Cycle.* Ballantine Books.

Narayan, K. (2012). *Alive in the Writing: Crafting Ethnography in the Company of Chekhov.* University of Chicago Press.

Nawijn, J., Marchand, M. A., Veenhoven, R., & Vingerhoets, A. J. (2010). Vacationers happier, but most not happier after a holiday. *Applied Research in Quality of Life, 5*(1), 35–47. https://doi.org/10.1007/s11482-009-9091-9

Nonaka, I. (1991). The knowledge creating company. *Harvard Business Review, 69,* 96–104.

Nzinga, S. M. (2020). *Lean Semesters: How Higher Education Reproduces Inequity.* Johns Hopkins University Press.

Olson, G. A., Faigley, L., & Chomsky, N. (1991). Language, politics, and composition: A conversation with Noam Chomsky. *Journal of Advanced Composition, 11*(1), 1–35.

Page, M. (2010, September). *Who Took the Sabbath out of Sabbatical?* AAUP. Retrieved April 11, 2022, from https://www.aaup.org/article/who-took-sabbath-out-sabbatical

Paltridge, B. (2002). Thesis and Dissertation Writing: An Examination of Published Advice and Actual Practice. *English for Specific Purposes, 21*(2), 125–143. https://doi.org/10.1016/s0889-4906(00)00025-9

Pang, A. S.-K. (2016). *Rest: Why You Get More Done When You Work Less.* Basic Books.

Peet, M. R. (n.d.). *The Integrative Knowledge Portfolio Process: A Guide for Educating Reflective Practitioners and Lifelong Learners.*

Pennycook, G., & Thompson, V. (2018). An analysis of the Canadian cognitive psychology job market (2006–2016). *Canadian Journal of Experimental Psychology/ Revue Canadienne De Psychologie Expérimentale, 72*(2), 71–80. https://doi.org/10.31234/osf.io/mxa35

Perrow, M., Feldstein, M., and Sieler, A. (2020). Ocean swimmer, woodchopper, road tripper: Using metaphor to develop students' identities as writers. *Journal of Adolescent & Adult Literacy, 64*(1), 37–46.

Perry, S. K. (1999). *Writing in Flow: Keys to Enhanced Creativity.* Writer's Digest Books.

Popova, M. (2015, October 5). *Famous Writers' Sleep Habits vs. Literary Productivity, Visualized.* The Marginalian. Retrieved April 4, 2022, from https://www.themarginalian.org/2013/12/16/writers-wakeup-times-literary-productivity-visualization/

Pyne, S. J. (2009). *Voice and Vision: A Guide to Writing History and Other Serious Nonfiction.* Harvard University Press.

Reinero, D. A. (2019, October 23). Is it publish or perish? The path to professorship by the numbers and why mentorship matters. *Nature News.* Retrieved April 12, 2022, from https://socialsciences.nature.com/posts/55118-the-path-to-professorship-by-the-numbers-and-why-mentorship-matters

Richardson, L. (1994). Writing: A method of inquiry. In N. K. Denzin & Y. S. Lincoln (Eds.), *Handbook of Qualitative Research* (pp. 516–529). SAGE Publications.

Rockquemore, K., & Laszloffy, T. A. (2008). *The Black Academic's Guide to Winning Tenure—Without Losing Your Soul.* Lynne Rienner Publishers.

Roney, L. (2017, December 13). *What Do Professors Do All Day? (I've Been Trying to Answer Most of My Life)*. University of Central Florida News | UCF Today. Retrieved April 5, 2022, from https://www.ucf.edu/news/what-do-professors-do-all-day/

Rose, M. (1984). *Writer's Block: The Cognitive Dimension*. Southern Illinois University Press.

Schön, D. A. (2016). *The Reflective Practitioner: How Professionals Think in Action*. Routledge.

Schoorman, D. (2021). Navigating identity and consciousness as an "outsider": Professional integration at the intersections of gender, nationality, and critical Scholarship. In M. Barakat and M. Rodríguez (Eds.), *Immigrant Faculty in the Academy: Narratives of Identity, Resilience, and Action*. Routledge.

Seamons, S. (2019, February 4). *Do College Professors Really Work 60-Hour Weeks?* Medium. Retrieved April 5, 2022, from https://medium.com/goreact-easy-video-feedback/do-college-professors-really-work-60-hour-weeks-5e3e7c1f5d14

Shahjahan, R. (2014). Being "lazy" and slowing down: Toward decolonizing time, our body, and pedagogy. *Educational Philosophy and Theory: Incorporating ACCESS*, 488–501.

Sharples, M. (1999). *How We Write: Writing as Creative Design*. Routledge.

Silvia, P. J. (2007). *How to Write a Lot: A Practical Guide to Productive Academic Writing*. APA LifeTools.

Smith, J. M. (2012). *An Absorbing Errand: How Artists and Craftsmen Make their Way to Mastery*. Counterpoint.

Strayed, C. (2012). *Tiny Beautiful Things: Advice on Love and Life from Dear Sugar*. Vintage Books.

Sword, H. (2012). *Stylish Academic Writing*. Harvard University Press.

Sword, H. (2017). *Air & Light & Time & Space: How Successful Academics Write*. Harvard University Press.

Sword, H. (2019). Snowflakes, splinters, and cobblestones: Metaphors for writing. In S. Farquhar & E. Fitzgerald (Eds.). *Innovations in Narrative and Metaphor: Methodologies and Practices*, 39–55. https://doi.org/10.1007/978-981-13-6114-2_4

Sword, H. (2023). *Writing with Pleasure*. Princeton University Press.

Tharp, T., & Reiter, M. (2003). *The Creative Habit: Learn It and Use It for Life*. Simon & Schuster.

Thesen, L., & Cooper, L. (Eds.). (2014). *Risk in Academic Writing: Postgraduate Students, their Teachers and the Making of Knowledge*. Multilingual Matters.

Torrance, M., & Galbraith, D. (2006). The processing demands of writing. In C. A. MacArthur, S. Graham, & J. Fitzgerald (Eds.), *Handbook of Writing Research* (pp. 67–80). The Guilford Press.

Usher, R. (2002). A diversity of doctorates: Fitness for the knowledge economy? *Higher Education Research & Development, 21*(2), 143–153. https://doi.org/10.1080/07294360220144060

Wagner, R. K., & Sternberg, R. J. (1985). Practical intelligence in real-world Pursuits: The role of tacit knowledge. *Journal of Personality and Social Psychology, 49*(2), 436–458. https://doi.org/10.1037/0022-3514.49.2.436

Warren, J. (2019). How much do you have to publish to get a job in a top sociology department? or to get tenure? Trends over a generation. *Sociological Science, 6,* 172–196. https://doi.org/10.15195/v6.a7

Weeks, K. (2011). *The Problem with Work: Feminism, Marxism, Antiwork Politics, and Postwork Imaginaries.* Duke University Press.

Wynne, C., Guo, Y.-J., & Wang, S.-C. (2014). Writing anxiety groups: A creative approach for graduate students. *Journal of Creativity in Mental Health, 9*(3), 366–379. https://doi.org/10.1080/15401383.2014.902343

Young, V. (2011). *The Secret Thoughts of Successful Women: Why Capable People Suffer from the Impostor Syndrome and How to Thrive in Spite of It.* Currency.

Zerubavel, E. (1999). *The Clockwork Muse: A Practical Guide to Writing Theses, Dissertations, and Books.* Harvard University Press.

Zimmerman, B. & Kitsantas, A. (2002). Acquiring writing revision and self-regulatory skill through observation and emulation. *Journal of Educational Psychology, 94*(4), 660–668.

Zumbrunn, S. K. (2021). *Why Aren't You Writing?: Research, Real Talk, Strategies, & Shenanigans.* SAGE Publications.

• Index •